Laying Down the Rails
for Children

A Habit-Training Companion

Book 2

by Lanaya Gore

Excerpts from Charlotte Mason's books are surrounded by quotation marks and accompanied by a reference to which book in the series they came from.
Vol. 1: Home Education
Vol. 2: Parents and Children
Vol. 3: School Education
Vol. 4: Ourselves
Vol. 5: Formation of Character
Vol. 6: A Philosophy of Education

Laying Down the Rails for Children: A Habit-Training Companion
© 2013 by Lanaya Gore

Cover Design: John Shafer

ISBN 978-1-61634-217-3 printed
ISBN 978-1-61634-218-0 electronic download

Published and printed in two volumes by
Simply Charlotte Mason, LLC
930 New Hope Road #11-892
Lawrenceville, Georgia 30045
United States

SimplyCharlotteMason.com

Contents

Book 2
Moral Habits

Physical Habits

Religious Habits

Moral Habits

Integrity

Firm adherence to a code of values;
being a good steward of all that we possess

Integrity in Priorities

Parent Prep

Read detailed thoughts about Integrity on pages 92–96 of *Laying Down the Rails* and skim the lessons below.

♦ Goals for this Habit (and steps to get there)

_____

_____

_____

♦ A Person or Story from My Life that Demonstrates this Habit

_____

_____

_____

♦ Additional Stories, Poems, Quotations, Bible Verses I Want to Use

_____

_____

_____

♦ Other Activities We Could Do to Practice this Habit

_____

_____

_____

♦ Celebration Ideas

_____

_____

_____

Choose the best way for your family to work through the habits in this book: 1) Pick and choose what seems most needed; 2) First do the top three recommended by Charlotte Mason— obedience, attention, and truthfulness; 3) Go through them in the order presented here in the book; 4) Rotate through the five categories—decency and propriety, mental, moral, physical, and religious— selecting one from each category in its turn.

Integrity is demonstrated in four specific areas of life: priorities, finishing what you start, use of time, and how you handle borrowed property.

Notes

Lesson 1

Read the definition for Integrity and discuss Priorities. Share with the children any goals you've identified for this habit (for instance, "We will finish schoolwork and chores and enjoy the outdoors before we have any screen [TV, computer, etc.] time."). Also get their input on changes they think need to be made.

Read the Biblical principle found in 1 Timothy 5:3–10 and verse 16 from your preferred version of the Bible. Families were to support their grandparents and parents instead of leaving them to burden the church. The church's priority was to be those widows who had no one to support them. Widows were to exhibit lives of integrity and be known for their good deeds.

Lesson 2

Talk over point one, helping your children to see that they can begin prioritizing for themselves even when they are young. Read and discuss "The Ant and the Cricket" to illustrate this point.

 1. Learn how to set priorities and practice prioritizing your work.

There is much prompting for discussion in these lessons. Be careful not to talk too much. Ask questions and listen to your children's thoughts.

The Ant and the Cricket
from *Fairy Stories and Fables* by James Baldwin

A silly young Cricket, who did nothing but sing through the warm sunny months of summer and spring, was sadly surprised when he found that at home his cupboard was empty, and winter had come. Not a crumb could be found on the snow-covered ground; not a flower could he see; not a leaf on a tree.

"Oh, what will become," said the Cricket, "of me?"

At last the poor Cricket, by hunger made bold, all dripping with wet, and all trembling with cold, to the house of an Ant went begging for food.

"Dear Ant," he began, "will you not be so good as to help a poor fellow, who has nothing to eat? I want a coat for my back, and shoes for my feet, a shelter from the rain, and a mouthful of grain. I wish only to borrow, I will pay you tomorrow—without them I must die of hunger and sorrow."

Said the Ant to the Cricket, "Do you know, my good friend, that we Ants never borrow, we Ants never lend? But tell me, I pray, did you lay nothing by when the weather was warm?"

Said the Cricket, "Not I! My heart was so light that I sang day and night, for all things looked gay."

"You sang, sir, you say? Go then," said the Ant, "and dance winter away."

Then, slamming the door in the poor Cricket's face, he went and sat down in his warm, cozy place, and said: "I am sure I'd be very, very poor if I idled away every warm summer day; and I think that this rule is both right and good, he who lives without work must go without food."

Lesson 3

Love God. Love your neighbor. This is the essence of all the commandments (Mark 12:28–31).

Read Matthew 15:1–20. Jesus removed heavy burdens when he discoursed about clean

■ Habit points from *Laying Down the Rails*

and unclean. Added-on rules and traditions had become more important than actually keeping one's heart and mind pure. Jesus declared the heart of the matter.

Lesson 4

Read and discuss "A Time to Talk." Yes, work must be completed; but use wisdom to know when to take a break for a more important situation that comes up in the midst of chores.

A Time to Talk
by Robert Frost

When a friend calls to me from the road
And slows his horse to a meaning walk,
I don't stand still and look around
On all the hills I haven't hoed,
And shout from where I am, What is it?
No, not as there is a time to talk.
I thrust my hoe in the mellow ground,
Blade-end up and five feet tall,
And plod: I go up to the stone wall
For a friendly visit.

Lesson 5

Read and discuss the quotation below. Make sure the children realize who A. A. Milne was (author of *Winnie the Pooh*).

"Organizing is what you do before you do something, so that when you do it, it's not all mixed up." — A. A. Milne

Activity: Have your children make a list of activities in their life. These can be things that need to be done as well as want-to activities. You can have them focus on a week, month, or year. Then help them prioritize the list by putting them in order of importance. You could do this activity as a family instead and focus on field trips, service projects, sports, special time spent with individual children, etc.

Lesson 6

Read and discuss the story below. Possessions often become a measure of value. There are many, many more important priorities in life than the coolness of your bicycle or the number of tech gadgets you own.

Socrates and His House
from *Fifty Famous Stories Retold* by James Baldwin

There once lived in Greece a very wise man whose name was Socrates. Young men from all parts of the land went to him to learn wisdom from him; and he said so many pleasant things, and said them in so delightful a way, that no one ever grew tired of listening to him.

One summer he built himself a house, but it was so small that his neighbors wondered how he could be content with it.

"What is the reason," said they, "that you, who are so great a man, should build such a little box as this for your dwelling house?"

"Indeed, there may be little reason," said he; "but, small as the place is, I shall think myself happy if I can fill even it with true friends."

Lesson 7

Following God gives meaning to our life. If God is not in it, our life becomes a chasing after the wind.

Read Ecclesiastes 11:7—12:14. Wise words are given to remember your Creator while you are young. Every action counts and is seen by God. The admonition at the end of the passage speaks to prioritizing.

Lesson 8

Matthew 6:33 tells us that our physical needs (food and clothing) will be met if we seek God's kingdom and righteousness first.

Have a Parent Share moment to share a story from your life or tell about a person who exemplifies Prioritizing.

Lesson 9

Remember to take a break and enjoy the little things in life. Children are usually great at this. Let them talk about some of the little things they enjoy. Read and discuss the poem below.

Barter

by Sara Teasdale

Life has loveliness to sell,
  All beautiful and splendid things,
Blue waves whitened on a cliff,
  Soaring fire that sways and sings,
And children's faces looking up,
Holding wonder like a cup.

Life has loveliness to sell,
  Music like the curve of gold,
Scent of pine trees in the rain,
  Eyes that love you, arms that hold,
And for your spirit's still delight,
Holy thoughts that star the night.

Spend all you have for loveliness,
  Buy it and never count the cost;
For one white singing hour of peace
  Count many a year of strife well lost,
And for a breath of ecstasy
Give all you have been, or could be.

Lesson 10

Prioritizing involves wisdom and forethought about the future. Don't let others persuade you to think only of the moment, especially if they have much to gain by their persuasion. Read and discuss "Mr. Vinegar and His Fortune."

Mr. Vinegar and His Fortune
from *Another Fairy Reader* by James Baldwin

I

A long time ago there lived a poor man whose real name has been forgotten. He was little and old, and his face was wrinkled; and that is why his friends called him Mr. Vinegar.

His wife was also little and old; and they lived in a little old cottage at the back of a little old field.

One day when Mrs. Vinegar was sweeping, she swept so hard that the little old door of the cottage fell down.

She was frightened. She ran out into the field and cried, "John! John! The house is falling down. We shall have no shelter over our heads."

Mr. Vinegar came and looked at the door.

Then he said, "Don't worry about that, my dear. Put on your bonnet and we will go out and seek our fortune."

So Mrs. Vinegar put on her hat, and Mr. Vinegar put the door on his head and they started.

They walked and walked all day. At night they came to a dark forest where there were many tall trees.

"Here is a good place to lodge," said Mr. Vinegar.

So he climbed a tree and laid the door across some branches. Then Mrs. Vinegar climbed the tree, and the two laid themselves down on the door.

"It is better to have the house under us than over us," said Mr. Vinegar. But Mrs. Vinegar was fast asleep, and did not hear him.

Soon it was pitch dark, and Mr. Vinegar also fell asleep. At midnight he was awakened by hearing a noise below him.

He started up. He listened.

"Here are ten gold pieces for you, Jack," he heard some one say; "and here are ten pieces for you, Bill. I'll keep the rest for myself."

Mr. Vinegar looked down. He saw three men sitting on the ground. A lighted lantern was near them.

"Robbers!" he cried in great fright, and sprang to a higher branch.

As he did this he kicked the door from its resting place. The door fell crashing to the ground, and Mrs. Vinegar fell with it.

The robbers were so badly scared that they took to their heels and ran helter-skelter into the dark woods.

"Are you hurt, my dear?" asked Mr. Vinegar.

"Ah, no!" said his wife. "But who would have thought the door would tumble down in the night? And here is a beautiful lantern, all lit and burning, to show us where we are."

Mr. Vinegar scrambled to the ground. He picked up the lantern to look at it. But what were those shining things that he saw lying all around?

"Gold pieces! gold pieces!" he cried; and he picked one up and held it to the light.

"We've found our fortune! We've found our fortune!" cried Mrs. Vinegar; and she jumped up and down for joy.

They gathered up the gold pieces. There were fifty of them, all bright and yellow and round.

"How lucky we are!" said Mr. Vinegar.

"How lucky we are!" said Mrs. Vinegar.

Then they sat down and looked at the gold till morning.

"Now, John," said Mrs. Vinegar, "I'll tell you what we'll do. You must go to the town and buy a cow. I will milk her and churn butter, and we shall never want for anything."

"That is a good plan," said Mr. Vinegar.

So he started off to the town, while his wife waited by the roadside.

II

Mr. Vinegar walked up and down the street of the town, looking for a cow. After a time a farmer came that way, leading one that was very pretty and fat.

"Oh, if I only had that cow," said Mr. Vinegar, "I would be the happiest man in the world."

"She is a very good cow," said the farmer.

"Well," said Mr. Vinegar, "I will give you these fifty gold pieces for her."

The farmer smiled and held out his hand for the money. "You may have her," he said. "I always like to oblige my friends."

Mr. Vinegar took hold the cow's halter and led her up and down the street. "I am the luckiest man in the world," he said, "for only see how all the people are looking at me and my cow."

But at the end of the street he met a man playing bagpipes. He stopped and listened. Tweedle-dee, tweedle-dee!

"Oh, that is the sweetest music I ever heard," he said. "And just see how all the children crowd around the man and give him pennies! If I only had those bagpipes, I would be the happiest man in the world."

"I will sell them to you," said the piper.

"Will you? Well then, since I have no money, I will give you this cow for them."

"You may have them," answered the piper. "I always like to oblige a friend."

Mr. Vinegar took the bagpipes, and the piper led the cow away.

"Now we will have some music," said Mr. Vinegar; but try as hard as he might, he could not play a tune. He could get nothing out of the bagpipes but "squeak! squeak!"

The children instead of giving him pennies, laughed at him. The day was chilly, and, in trying to play the pipes, his fingers grew very cold. He wished that he had kept the cow.

He had just started for home when he met a man who had warm gloves on his hands. "Oh, if I only had those pretty gloves," he said, "I would be the happiest man in the world."

"How much will you give for them?" asked the man.

"I have no money, but I will give you these bagpipes," answered Mr. Vinegar.

"Well," said the man, "you may have them; for I always like to oblige a friend."

Mr. Vinegar gave him the bagpipes and drew the gloves on over his half-frozen fingers. "How lucky I am!" he said, as he trudged homeward.

His hands were soon quite warm; but the road was rough and the walking hard. He was very tired when he came to the foot of a steep hill.

"How shall I ever get to the top?" he said.

Just then he met a man who was walking the other way. He had a stick in his hand which he used as a cane to help him along.

"My friend," said Mr. Vinegar, "if I only had that stick of yours to help me up this hill, I would be the happiest man in the world."

"How much will you give me for it?" asked the man.

"I have no money, but I will give you this pair of warm gloves," said Mr. Vinegar.

"Well," said the man, "you may have it; for I always like to oblige a friend."

Mr. Vinegar's hands were now quite warm. So he gave the gloves to the man and took the stout stick to help him along.

"How lucky I am," he said, as he toiled upward.

At the top of the hill he stopped to rest. But as he was thinking of all his good luck that day, he heard some one calling his name. He looked up and saw only a green parrot sitting in a tree.

"Mr. Vinegar! Mr. Vinegar!" it cried.

"What now?" asked Mr. Vinegar.

"You're a dunce! You're a dunce!" answered the bird. "You went to seek your fortune, and you found it. Then you gave it for a cow, and the cow for some bagpipes, and the bagpipes for some gloves, and the gloves for a stick which you might have cut by the roadside. He! he! he! he! he! You're a dunce! You're a dunce!"

This made Mr. Vinegar very angry. He threw the stick at the bird with all his might. But the bird only answered. "You're a dunce! You're a dunce!" and the stick lodged in the tree where he could not get it again.

Mr. Vinegar went home slowly, for he had many things to think about. His wife was standing by the roadside, and as soon as she saw him she cried out, "Where's the cow? Where's the cow?"

"Well, I don't just know where the cow is," said Mr. Vinegar; and then he told her the whole story.

I have heard said that she gave him a sound beating; but it is best not to believe such tales.

"We are no worse off than we were yesterday," said Mr. Vinegar. "Let us go home and take care of our little old house."

Then he put the door on his head and trudged onward. And Mrs. Vinegar followed him.

Lesson 11

Talk about ways to put the Lord first.

Read Haggai chapter 1. The Lord exhorted the people of Israel to rebuild His house first instead of leaving it in ruins and working on their own homes.

Lesson 12

Finish up with any other discussion, ideas, or celebration your family enjoys. Keep up this habit while going forth to concentrate on a new one.

Activity: Put a scavenger hunt together for the children to work on as a team or separately. Assign different amounts of points to each item they need to find, but do not arrange the items in order of points. Let the children decide which items should take priority in their search to accumulate a good score. You could award levels of prizes for the number of points found within a time limit: candy bar for 5 points found; pool time for 10 points found; day off of school for 50 points found, etc.

Integrity in Finishing

Parent Prep

Read detailed thoughts about Integrity on pages 92–96 of *Laying Down the Rails* and skim the lessons below.

- ◆ Goals for this Habit (and steps to get there)

_____

_____

_____

- ◆ A Person or Story from My Life that Demonstrates this Habit

_____

_____

_____

- ◆ Additional Stories, Poems, Quotations, Bible Verses I Want to Use

_____

_____

_____

- ◆ Other Activities We Could Do to Practice this Habit

_____

_____

_____

- ◆ Celebration Ideas

_____

_____

_____

Lesson 1

Read the definition for Integrity (below) and relate it to Finishing. Share with the children any goals you've identified for this habit (for instance, "We will not make promises to complete something within a timeframe that we cannot keep."). Also get their input on changes they think need to be made.

Integrity – Firm adherence to a code of values; being a good steward of all that we possess

Read the Biblical principle found in 2 Timothy 4:6–8 from your preferred version of the Bible. It's a rousing reminiscence of Paul's keeping the faith until the very end. Finishing our race of faith well is the most important thing in life we could finish.

Lesson 2

Discuss with your children point two and the quotation below. Young children can begin practicing this habit by putting away toys before moving to another area of play.

 2. Finish one project before beginning something new.

"There is nothing so fatal to character as half-finished tasks." — *David Lloyd George*

Lesson 3

A most essential quality of Finishing is being faithful unto death. Read and discuss a historical example of this quality in "Faithful Till Death."

Faithful Till Death
adapted from *A Book of Golden Deeds* by Charlotte M. Yonge

Rudolf von der Wart woefully fell in with a group who conspired and subsequently murdered Emperor Albrecht I of Hapsburg. The family sought vengeance upon the murderers and their kinsmen, and though Rudolf had not participated in the murder, he was sentenced to a slow, painful death. The hero of this story though is his wife Gertrude. She faithfully stood by him until his last breaths.

Rudolf von der Wart received the horrible sentence of being broken on the wheel. On his trial the Emperor's attendant declared that Der Wart had attacked Albert with his dagger, and the cry, 'How long will ye suffer this carrion to sit on horseback?' but he persisted to the last that he had been taken by surprise by the murder. However, there was no mercy for him; and, by the express command of Queen Agnes, his sentence was carried out and he was set upon a pole, where he was to linger out the remaining hours of his life. His young wife, Gertrude, who had clung to him through all the trial, was torn away and carried off to the Castle of Kyburg; but she made her escape at dusk, and found her way, as night came on, to the spot where her husband hung still living upon the wheel. That night of agony was described in a letter ascribed to Gertrude herself. The guard left to watch fled at her approach, and she prayed beneath the scaffold, and then, heaping some heavy logs of wood together, was able to climb up near enough to embrace him and stroke back the hair from his face, whilst he entreated her to leave him, lest she should be found there, and fall under the cruel revenge of the Queen, telling her that thus it would be possible to increase his suffering.

'I will die with you,' she said, ''tis for that I came, and no power shall force me from you;' and she prayed for the one mercy she hoped for, speedy death for her husband.

> In Mrs. Hemans' beautiful words—
> 'And bid me not depart,' she cried,
> 'My Rudolf, say not so;
> This is no time to quit thy side,
> Peace, peace, I cannot go!
> Hath the world aught for me to fear
> When death is on thy brow?
> The world! what means it? Mine is here!
> I will not leave thee now.

Parental Discretion Advisory: This story may be too intense for some children. As always, use discretion and wisdom in determining whether it is appropriate for your family members.

📖 Habit points from *Laying Down the Rails*

'I have been with thee in thine hour
Of glory and of bliss;
Doubt not its memory's living power
To strengthen me through this.
And thou, mine honor'd love and true,
Bear on, bear nobly on;
We have the blessed heaven in view,
Whose rest shall soon be won.'

When day began to break, the guard returned, and Gertrude took down her stage of wood and continued kneeling at the foot of the pole. Crowds of people came to look, among them the wife of one of the officials, whom Gertrude implored to intercede that her husband's sufferings might be ended; but though this might not be, some pitied her, and tried to give her wine and confections, which she could not touch. The priest came and exhorted Rudolf to confess the crime, but with a great effort he repeated his former statement of innocence.

A band of horsemen rode by. Among them was the young Prince Leopold and his sister Agnes herself, clad as a knight. They were very angry at the compassion shown by the crowd, and after frightfully harsh language commanded that Gertrude should be dragged away; but one of the nobles interceded for her, and when she had been carried away to a little distance her entreaties were heard, and she was allowed to break away and come back to her husband. The priest blessed Gertrude, gave her his hand and said, 'Be faithful unto death, and God will give you the crown of life,' and she was no further molested.

Night came on, and with it a stormy wind, whose howling mingled with the voice of her prayers, and whistled in the hair of the sufferer. One of the guard brought her a cloak. She climbed on the wheel, and spread the covering over her husband's limbs; then fetched some water in her shoe, and moistened his lips with it, sustaining him above all with her prayers, and exhortations to look to the joys beyond. He had ceased to try to send her away, and thanked her for the comfort she gave him. And still she watched when morning came again, and noon passed over her, and it was verging to evening, when for the last time he moved his head; and she raised herself so as to be close to him. With a smile, he murmured, 'Gertrude, this is faithfulness till death,' and died. She knelt down to thank God for having enabled her to remain for that last breath—

'While even as o'er a martyr's grave
She knelt on that sad spot,
And, weeping, blessed the God who gave
Strength to forsake it not!'

She found shelter in a convent at Basle, where she spent the rest of her life in a quiet round of prayer and good works; till the time came when her widowed heart should find its true rest for ever.

Lesson 4

Read and discuss the poem, "The Oak." Completing tasks and school assignments and keeping promises helps one stand tall and strong.

The Oak
by Alfred Lord Tennyson

Live thy Life,
   Young and old,
Like yon oak,
Bright in spring,
   Living gold;

Summer-rich
   Then; and then
Autumn-changed
Soberer-hued
   Gold again.

All his leaves
   Fall'n at length,
Look, he stands,
Trunk and bough
   Naked strength.

Lesson 5

Read and discuss the quotation.

> *"Genius begins great works; labor alone finishes them."* — *Joseph Joubert*

Read Nehemiah 6:15—7:3. Amidst trials and after much hard work, the men completed the rebuilding of the walls around Jerusalem.

Lesson 6

Read and discuss the quotation.

> *"Do not plan for ventures before finishing what's at hand."* — *Euripides*

Activity: Have the children make butter by filling a jar about half full with room temperature heavy cream and adding a pinch or two of salt. They can take turns shaking the jar or rolling it to one another. Make it fun with music or jumping activities. This will take some time (about 30 minutes) and perseverance, but encourage them to finish the job. Once a good lump has formed, rinse it with cold water to remove the buttermilk. Provide bread (homemade would be delicious!) or toast or muffins to spread their butter on. Refrigerate any leftover butter.

Lesson 7

Discuss how fulfilling one's duty relates to Integrity and Finishing. The story, "About Dogs," gives an illustration of this point.

About Dogs
from *Harper's Third Reader*, edited by James Baldwin

What creature is more faithful to its master than the dog? In the cold lands of the North, where he is used to draw sleds over the ice and snow; in the great cities, where he watches his master's goods and house; in the fields, taking care of flocks and herds; in the woods, chasing the deer or facing the fierce wild beasts—all over the world the dog is man's best friend.

I once knew a fine shepherd dog named Fanny, who took care of a large flock of sheep on a sheep farm in the far West. Every morning she drove the sheep out upon the prairie where they were allowed to feed on the grass; and every evening she brought them safe home and saw them shut up in the sheep barn.

One day there came up a blinding storm of snow and sleet while the sheep were feeding far away from any shelter. Fanny gathered them together as best she could, and tried to drive them home. But they were so cold and frightened that they did not know what to do.

Now they would huddle close together, and would not move at all; now some of them would scamper wildly away over the hills; and faithful Fanny had hard work to get them started on the right road.

It was very late that evening when the sheep came home. They were all wet and wretched; and Fanny was wet and tired too, but proud that she had succeeded in bringing them in from the pasture.

"Well, Fanny," said her master, "here you are with your flock! How many have you lost?"

The sheep were counted as they passed into the barnyard.

"Three lambs missing, Fanny," said her master. "You have done well not to lose more."

But Fanny did not want to hear the last words. She understood that three lambs were missing, and wet and tired and hungry as she was, she bounded away in search of them. Her master called to her to come back; but she did not hear. The storm became worse and worse. The snow fell fast and the wind piled it up into great heaps or sent it flying in blinding gusts through the air.

We sat up until very late that night, waiting for poor Fanny, but she did not come. At last we gave her up as lost; for we did not think that any creature could live out on the prairie in that terrible storm.

Just at the peep of day next morning we heard a faint bark outside the barnyard. We looked out, and there was Fanny with the three lambs. She was so worn out with her long search in the storm that she could hardly drag herself through the snow.

But her eyes sparkled when she looked at us, as if she would say: "I have done my duty and saved the lambs." We took her into the house and cared for her as we would have cared for a human being; but it was a long, long time before she was strong enough to drive her flock out to pasture upon the prairies again.

Lesson 8

Read and discuss the quotation below, then have a Parent Share moment to share a story from your life or tell about a person who exemplifies Finishing.

"Promises must be kept, deadlines met, commitments honored, not for the sake of morality, but because we become what we do or fail to do. Character is the sum of all that." — Howard Sparks

Lesson 9

Share and enjoy the illustrative quotation below.

"There are two kinds of people, those who finish what they start and so on." — *Robert Byrne*

Activity: Play a game in which the children have to get at missing pieces in order to finish. You could

1. Freeze pennies inside ice cubes. Give 10 unfrozen pennies to the children and tell them they have to toss 15 into a can from a distance away. They will eventually get the 10 in and notice they are missing some pennies. Give them the frozen ice cubes of pennies and let them unfreeze them in any way they think of in order to finish the game.

or

2. Freeze a puzzle piece. (It will be a little wet, but does not incur substantial damage once dried. You could also put it in a sandwich bag and freeze it in a bowl.) The children can put together the puzzle to discover that one piece is missing. Give them the frozen piece to thaw out and finish the puzzle.

Lesson 10

Finish up with any other discussion, ideas, or celebration your family enjoys. Keep up this habit while going forth to concentrate on a new one.

Integrity in Use of Time

Parent Prep

Read detailed thoughts about Integrity on pages 92–96 of *Laying Down the Rails* and skim the lessons below.

♦ Goals for this Habit (and steps to get there)

_____

_____

_____

♦ A Person or Story from My Life that Demonstrates this Habit

_____

_____

_____

♦ Additional Stories, Poems, Quotations, Bible Verses I Want to Use

_____

_____

_____

♦ Other Activities We Could Do to Practice this Habit

_____

_____

_____

_____

♦ Celebration Ideas

_____

_____

_____

As you work through these lessons with your children, you are also training yourself to be a habit trainer and to develop these habits while giving your children much to contemplate and to inspire them.

Lesson 1

Read the definition below for Integrity and discuss how it relates to Use of Time. Share with the children any goals you've identified for this habit (for instance, "At the end of each day, we will name at least one accomplishment with which we can be satisfied as we lay our heads down to rest."). Also get their input on changes they think need to be made.

Integrity – Firm adherence to a code of values; being a good steward of all that we possess

Read the Biblical principle found in Titus 3:14 from your preferred version of the Bible. A productive life consists of providing for daily necessities and doing what is good.

Lesson 2

Talk about point three evaluating how your family does with this principle. Read and discuss the poem by Isaac Watts below.

 3. Make good use of your time every day.

Against Idleness and Mischief
by Isaac Watts

How doth the little busy bee
   Improve each shining hour,
And gather honey all the day
   From every opening flower!

How skilfully she builds her cell!
   How neat she spreads the wax!
And labours hard to store it well
   With the sweet food she makes.

In works of labour or of skill
   I would be busy too;
For Satan finds some mischief still
   For idle hands to do.

In books, or work, or healthful play
   Let my first years be past,
That I may give for every day
   Some good account at last.

Lesson 3

Working smart is as important as working hard.

Read Exodus 18:13–26. Upon Jethro's advice, Moses lightened his daily workload while accomplishing more. Acts 6:1–7 is also a good example of spreading the workload; the apostles delegated some tasks to capable men in order to free up time for the apostles to do specialized work for the church.

Lesson 4

Read and discuss the quotations below. Make sure students know the position Margaret Thatcher held as Prime Minister of England and can appreciate how many things she had to do during a day. Talk about the satisfaction that comes from a full day's work.

"Those who make the worst use of their time are the first to complain of its shortness."
— *Jean de La Bruyere*

"Look at a day when you are supremely satisfied at the end. It's not a day when you lounge around doing nothing. It's when you've had everything to do, and you've done it." — *Margaret Thatcher*

 Habit points from
Laying Down the Rails

Lesson 5

Ecclesiastes 11:9 brings up the principle of remembering God in the days of our youth because our actions will be brought to judgment. The way we choose to use our young years shapes us into the persons we will become as adults. Read and discuss "Grown-up Land."

Grown-up Land
from *Harper's Third Reader*, edited by James Baldwin

"Good-morrow, good-morrow, my bright-eyed lad,
Now what may your trouble be?"

"Good-morrow," he answered me, sober and sad;
"Here is sorrow enough for me.
Say, which is the road to Grown-up Land—
The shortest, kind stranger, I pray?
For these guideboards all point with different hand,
In a dreadfully puzzling way.
This says, By the Town of Saving a Cent;
Another, Just follow your Natural Bent;
This points to the Road of Wisely Giving;
And that to the Turnpike of Truly Living;
A fifth straggles off here to Leapfrog Town;
And the sixth climbs the mountain of High Renown;
These lead to the byways of Bat and Ball
And the highways of Courage and Know It All;
Then, there are the crossroads of Play and Fun,
And the post roads of Duty and Things Well Done.
Oh dear! how can a *boy* understand
Which way is the shortest to Grown-up Land?"

"Don't fret, my lad, for the roads, you see,
Have been traveled by many like you and me;
And, though each road has a different name,
To Grown-up Land they, all of them, came.
And hour by hour, my boy, you'll find
That, little by little they drop behind;
Till, almost before you know it, you stand
On the breezy hilltop of Grown-up Land."

"Good-morrow, my lassie, with face so sweet,
Where are you going with your flying feet?"

"Good-morrow," she answered, with wave of hand,
"I am off in a hurry to Grown-up Land.
But I wish you would show me the shortest way,
For these guideboards, I'm certain, will lead me astray.
Just think! one says, 'Tis a Stitch in Time;
And another, Through Smiles and Tears;
This says, It is only by Uphill Work;

And that, By the Flight of Years.
Another says, Play; and another, Books;
And another, Just Dance and Sing;
And this one says, Help; and that one, Hope;
And this, Care in the Smallest Thing.
Oh, the roads are so many! Who *can* understand
Which is the best way to Grown-up Land?"

"Don't worry, my lassie, with eyes so blue,
For whichever the road that is traveled by you
It will carry you forward until you stand
On the sunlit hilltops of Grown-up Land!"

And lassie and lad
Ran off in glee,
Without so much
As "Good-day" to me.
And in Grown-up Land,
Whatever their way,
They will meet together
On Big Folks' Day.

Lesson 6

In a world that can have you running from one thing to the next without ever stopping to enjoy the journey, we must remember that a balanced schedule, with time for rest as well as work, is essential. Read and discuss the poem below.

I Meant to Do My Work Today
by Richard Le Gallienne

I meant to do my work to-day—
But a brown bird sang in the apple-tree
And a butterfly flitted across the field,
And all the leaves were calling me.

And the wind went sighing over the land,
Tossing the grasses to and fro,
And a rainbow held out its shining hand—
So what could I do but laugh and go?

Lesson 7

Read and discuss the quotation below.

*"If a man has any greatness in him, it comes to light—not in one flamboyant hour,
but in the ledger of his daily work."* — *Beryl Markham*

Activity: Do a little exercise in which you pretend each child is given $1440 every day

Feed minds. Inspire hearts. Encourage action.

and ask him what he would do with it. Explain that we are each given 1440 minutes every day and discuss good ways to use it. Include restful, fun ideas for the end of the day when chores and have-to's are done.

Lesson 8

Read and discuss the quotation and story excerpt below.

> *"Never lose one moment of time, but improve it in the most profitable way possible."*
> — *Jonathan Edwards*

from *The Five Little Peppers and How They Grew*
by Margaret Sidney

"Shan't we ever have anything else to eat, Polly?" asked the child gravely, getting down from her high chair to watch the operation of cleaning the floor.

"Oh, yes," said Polly cheerfully, "lots and lots—when our ship comes in."

"What'll they be?" asked Phronsie, in the greatest delight, prepared for anything.

"Oh, I don't know," said Polly. "Ice cream for one thing, Phronsie, and maybe little cakes."

"With pink on top?" interrupted Phronsie, getting down by Polly's side.

"Oh, yes," said Polly, warming with her subject, "ever an' ever so much pink, Phronsie Pepper; more'n you could eat!"

.....

"Oh," cried Phronsie, "I want some now, I *do*!"

.....

"Your ships aren't ever coming in," broke in Mrs. Pepper wisely, "if you sit there talking. Folks don't ever make any fortunes by wishing."

Lesson 9

Read Psalm 90. Life on earth is short compared to eternity. It is short just comparing the years to earth's history. God makes the difference between a life that has real meaning and a life that leaves no true legacy.

Lesson 10

Read and discuss the quotation below. Make sure the children know who Theodore Roosevelt was and can appreciate the need for scheduling time as President.

> *"Nine-tenths of wisdom consists in being wise in scheduling time."* — *Theodore Roosevelt*

Activity: Plant some seeds or do some gardening or yard work. Talk about the hard work it takes to cultivate the beauty and food the comes from gardening and lawn beautification. Ask the children to think of rewards that come from diligent work and the consequences that come from poor work (weeds, ugly yard, puny produce). You could also simply visit a flower garden or enjoy fresh produce from a road stand.

Lesson 11

We cannot get those moments back that have passed, so wisdom should be used in how we spend each moment. Read and discuss the poem below.

The Water Mill

from *Harper's Third Reader*, edited by James Baldwin

Listen to the water mill;
    Through the livelong day
How the clanking of the wheels
    Wears the hours away!

Lazily the autumn wind
    Stirs the greenwood leaves,
While, in the fields, the reapers sing,
    Binding up the sheaves.

Then comes this saying to my mind—
    A saying true to the last—
"The mill will never, never grind
    With the water that has passed."

Take this lesson to yourself,
    And study it through and through;
For golden years are fleeting by,
    And youth is passing too.

Learn to make the most of life,
    Lose no happy day;
For time will never bring you back
    The moments thrown away.

Leave no tender word unsaid;
    And love while life shall last.
"The mill will never, never grind
    With the water that has passed."

Work while yet the daylight shines,
    Man of strength and will!
Never does the mill stream glide
    Vainly by the mill.

Wait not till to-morrow's sun
    Beams upon the way;
All that you can call your own
    Lies in your to-day.

Clear mind, strong body, youth and health,
    May not, cannot last;
"The mill will never, never grind
    With the water that has passed."

Lesson 12

Read and discuss the quotation below, then finish up with any other discussion, ideas, or celebration your family enjoys. Keep up this habit while going forth to concentrate on a new one.

"You will always be glad at evening if you have spent the day well." — *Thomas a Kempis*

Have a Parent Share moment to share a story from your life or tell about a person who exemplifies good Use of Time.

Integrity in Borrowed Property

Parent Prep

Read detailed thoughts about Integrity on pages 92–96 of *Laying Down the Rails* and skim the lessons below.

♦ Goals for this Habit (and steps to get there)

_____

_____

_____

♦ A Person or Story from My Life that Demonstrates this Habit

_____

_____

_____

♦ Additional Stories, Poems, Quotations, Bible Verses I Want to Use

_____

_____

_____

♦ Other Activities We Could Do to Practice this Habit

_____

_____

_____

♦ Celebration Ideas

_____

_____

_____

Lesson 1

Read the definition of Integrity below and discuss its relationship to Borrowed Property. Share with the children any goals you've identified for this habit (for instance, "We will establish rules on how to care for the library books we borrow."). Also get their input on changes they think need to be made.

Integrity - Firm adherence to a code of values; being a good steward of all that we possess

Read the command found in Deuteronomy 5:19 from your preferred version of the Bible. Be careful that you don't inadvertently steal from someone by not returning their property. If you choose to borrow from someone, show that you can be fully trusted by taking care of the item and returning it in a timely matter.

Lesson 2

Discuss point four. Talk about acceptable times to borrow and when to refrain from borrowing. Read and discuss the quotation below.

 4. Anything you borrow should be returned promptly and in good shape.

"A man can get a reputation from very small things." — *Sophocles*

Lesson 3

If you agree to care for someone else's property, be sure you can be responsible for it. Read and discuss the story below.

Maximillian and the Goose Boy
from *Fifty Famous Stories* by James Baldwin

One summer day King Maximilian of Bavaria was walking in the country. The sun shone hot, and he stopped under a tree to rest.

It was very pleasant in the cool shade. The king lay down on the soft grass, and looked up at the white clouds sailing across the sky. Then he took a little book from his pocket and tried to read.

But the king could not keep his mind on his book. Soon his eyes closed, and he was fast asleep.

It was past noon when he awoke. He got up from his grassy bed, and looked around. Then he took his cane in his hand, and started for home.

When he had walked a mile or more, he happened to think of his book. He felt for it in his pocket. It was not there. He had left it under the tree.

The king was already quite tired, and he did not like to walk back so far. But he did not wish to lose the book. What should he do?

If there was only someone to send for it!

While he was thinking, he happened to see a little bare-footed boy in the open field near the road. He was tending a large flock of geese that were picking the short grass, and wading in a shallow brook.

The king went toward the boy. He held a gold piece in his hand.

"My boy," he said, "how would you like to have this piece of money?"

"I would like it," said the boy; "but I never hope to have so much."

"You shall have it if you will run back to the oak tree at the second turning of the road, and fetch me the book that I left there."

The king thought that the boy would be pleased. But not so. He turned away, and said, "I am not so silly as you think."

"What do you mean?" said the king. "Who says that you are silly?"

"Well," said the boy, "you think that I am silly enough to believe that you will give me that gold piece for running a mile, and fetching you a book. You can't catch me."

"But if I give it to you now, perhaps you will believe me," said the king; and he put the gold piece into the little fellow's hand.

The boy's eyes sparkled; but he did not move.

"What is the matter now?" said the king. "Won't you go?"

The boy said, "I would like to go; but I can't leave the geese. They will stray away, and then I shall be blamed for it."

"Oh, I will tend them while you are away," said the king.

The boy laughed. "I should like to see you tending them!" he said. "Why, they would run away from you in a minute."

"Only let me try," said the king.

At last the boy gave the king his whip, and started off. He had gone but a little way, when he turned and came back.

"What is the matter now?" said Maximilian.

"Crack the whip!"

The king tried to do as he was bidden, but he could not make a sound.

"I thought as much," said the boy. "You don't know how to do anything."

Then he took the whip, and gave the king lessons in whip cracking. "Now you see how it is done," he said, as he handed it back. "If the geese try to run away, crack it loud."

The king laughed. He did his best to learn his lesson; and soon the boy again started off on his errand.

Maximilian sat down on a stone, and laughed at the thought of being a goose-herd. But the geese missed their master at once. With a great cackling and hissing they went, half flying, half running, across the meadow.

The king ran after them, but he could not run fast. He tried to crack the whip, but it was of no use. The geese were soon far away. What was worse, they had gotten into a garden, and were feeding on the tender vegetables.

A few minutes afterward, the goose boy came back with the book.

"Just as I thought," he said. "I have found the book, and you have lost the geese."

"Never mind," said the king, "I will help you get them again."

"Well, then, run around that way, and stand by the brook while I drive them out of the garden."

The king did as he was told. The boy ran forward with his whip, and after a great deal of shouting and scolding, the geese were driven back into the meadow.

"I hope you will pardon me for not being a better goose-herd," said Maximilian; "but, as I am a king, I am not used to such work."

"A king, indeed!" said the boy. "I was very silly to leave the geese with you. But I am not so silly as to believe that you are a king."

"Very well," said Maximilian, with a smile; "here is another gold piece, and now let us be friends."

The boy took the gold, and thanked the giver. He looked up into the king's face and said,—

"You are a very kind man, and I think you might be a good king; but if you were to try all your life, you would never be a good goose-herd."

Lesson 4

If borrowed property is stolen, broken, or lost, consider what you should do to make up the loss.

Read 2 Kings 6:1–7. A prophet (not a lucrative position) lost a borrowed axehead in an accident. God provided, though, and Elisha helped the prophet get it back.

Lesson 5

Library lending is a blessing and possibly one of the most capitalized-on forms of borrowing for your family.

Activity: Come up with some family rules for borrowing books from the library. You could write them on a poster or just keep them on a sheet of paper in the library bag.

- ♦ Will you have separate library cards or just one? Where will they be kept?
- ♦ Will you have one library bag or individual ones?
- ♦ What should you do if a page gets torn?
- ♦ Is there a book limit per child?
- ♦ May they eat or drink around the library books?
- ♦ Where will the library books be stored when not being read?
- ♦ Who will be responsible for a missing book?
- ♦ Who will be responsible for remembering when the library books are due?

Lesson 6

"The borrower is servant to the lender" (Proverbs 22:7). A lender must be careful also, because he is taking a risk. Read and discuss the story below. Though it is quite a fanciful story, it brings home the point of being wise in lending.

Drakesbill and His Friends
from Fairy Stories and Fables by James Baldwin

Drakesbill was very little, and that is why some people called him Bill Drake; but, tiny as he was, he knew a thing or two. He was a great worker and laid up every cent that he earned; and, long before he was half as tall as a gray goose, he had saved a hundred dollars in gold. The King of the country, who never did anything but spend money, heard that Drakesbill had some gold pieces, and he made haste to borrow them. How very kind and gracious he was until he heard the little yellow coins jingle in his pocket! And how proud it made Drakesbill feel to have it said that he had lent money to the King!

A year went by,—two years, three years,—and the King seemed to have forgotten him. He did not even offer to pay Drakesbill the interest, and the little fellow was very uneasy lest he should lose all his money. At last he made up his mind that he would go and see the King and tell him that he needed the gold pieces very much.

So, early one morning, Drakesbill, as spruce and fresh as a young robin, went down the high road towards the King's palace, singing, "Quack, quack, quack, when shall I get my money back?"

He had not gone far when he met friend Fox coming home from his rounds among the farm-yards.

"Good morning, my good neighbor," said friend Fox; "where are you going so early in the day?"

"I am going to the King to ask him to pay me what he owes me."

"Oh! take me with you!"

"One can't have too many friends," thought Drakesbill. Then he said, "Certainly I will take you; but you walk on four legs, and you will soon get tired. So make yourself very small, get into my mouth, creep under my tongue—and I will carry you."

Friend Fox thanked him very kindly, made himself very small, and was out of sight like a letter in a letter box.

Then Drakesbill was off again, all spruce and fresh as a spring morning, and still singing, "Quack, quack, quack, when shall I get my money back?"

He had not gone far when he met his lady friend Ladder leaning against her wall.

"Good morning, ducky darling," said the lady friend, "whither away, so bold and gay, this fine, new day?"

"I am going to the King to ask him to pay me what he owes me."

"Oh! take me with you!"

"One can't have too many friends," thought Drakesbill. Then he said, "Certainly I will take you; but you have such long wooden legs that you will soon get tired. So make yourself very small, get into my mouth, creep under my tongue—and I will carry you."

The Ladder thanked him, made herself very small, and went to keep company with friend Fox.

Then Drakesbill was off again, spruce and fresh as any dapper little dandy, and singing, "Quack, quack, quack, when shall I get my money back?"

He had not gone far when he met his sweet-heart, laughing River, wandering quietly in the sunshine.

"Good morning, my spoon bill," she said, "whither do you go, so happy and slow, while the soft breezes blow?"

"I am going to the King, you know, for he owes me money, and I want him to pay me back."

"Oh! take me with you!"

"One can't have too many friends," thought Drakesbill. Then he said, "Certainly I will take you; but you always sleep while you run, and you will soon get tired. So make yourself very small, get into my mouth, creep under my tongue—and I will carry you."

The River thanked him very kindly, and then, glou! glou! glou! she went to take her place between friend Fox and friend Ladder.

And Drakesbill was off again, spruce and fresh as a busy bee, and singing "Quack, quack, quack, when shall I get my money back?"

A little farther on he met neighbor Wasp-nest, taking his wasps out for some fresh air.

"Good morning, neighbor Bill," said Wasp-nest; "whither do we run, so full of fun, in the bright, warm sun?"

"Oh, don't you know that the King owes me money? And I am going down to see him and make him pay me," answered Drakesbill.

"Oh! take us with you!"

"One can't have too many friends," thought Drakesbill. Then he said, "Certainly I will take you; but there are so many of you that you will soon get tired. So make yourself quite small, get into my mouth, creep under my tongue—and I will carry you."

Neighbor Wasp-nest thanked him very kindly, and then buzz, buzz, buzz, file right! march! There wasn't much more room, but by getting close together everybody was made quite comfortable.

And then Drakesbill went on singing.

In the afternoon he came to the great city where the King lived; and as he marched straight up High Street, he sang as loud as he could, "Quack quack, quack! Oh, when shall I get my money back?"

When he came to the King's palace he climbed up the step; and then he stood on tip-toe, and knocked at the door, toc! toc! toc!

"Who's there?" asked the doorkeeper, looking out through the keyhole.

" 'Tis I, Drakesbill. I want to speak with the King."

"Speak with the King? Nonsense. That is easier said than done. The King is in the parlor counting out his money."

"That is just what I want to see him do," said Drakesbill. "Tell him I am here, and then he will know my business."

The doorkeeper went into the parlor to speak with the King. But he was not there; he was in the kitchen, just sitting down to dinner with a white napkin round his neck.

"Good! good!" said the King. "I know the rascal. Fetch him in and put him with the turkeys and chickens."

The doorkeeper went back to the door.

"Walk in, sir!"

"Good!" said Drakesbill to himself. "Now I can see how the folks eat at the King's table."

"This way, this way!" said the doorkeeper. "Now step through that gate. There you are!"

"What! In the poultry yard? How? What?"

How vexed the little fellow was! And no wonder.

"Just wait," he said at last. "I think I'll show them a thing or two. Quack, quack, quack, when shall I get my money back?"

But turkeys and chickens are queer things, as you know, and think themselves a good deal better than other folks. When they saw what a funny little fellow had come among them, and when they heard him singing his queer song, they began to ask one another:

"Who is he? What is he doing here?"

Then they all rushed upon him, and if he had not had his wits about him they would have pecked him to death in no time. But, as good luck would have it, he remembered his friend Fox, and he cried out:—

"Fox, friend Fox, from your hiding place
Come quick, or sad will be my case!"

Then friend Fox, who was only waiting for these words, leaped out from his hiding place, as big as life and as happy as a sunflower; and he threw himself on the wicked fowls, and snip, snap! crish, crash! he tore them in pieces; and at the end of five minutes not one of them was left alive. And Drakesbill, spruce and fresh as ever, began to sing again, "Quack, quack, quack, when shall I get my money back?"

But the King was very angry when the poultry woman and the cook and the doorkeeper all rushed into the kitchen where he was eating and told him what had happened. He ordered them to seize this naughty little Drakesbill, and throw him into the well, and thus make an end of him.

"I am lost! I am lost!" cried Drakesbill as he fell fluttering down into the deep, dark hole. "I can never climb out of this place!"

Then he happened to think of his lady friend Ladder, and he sang:—

"Ladder, Ladder, from beneath my tongue
Come quick, or soon my song will be sung!"

Friend Ladder, who had only been waiting for these words, leaped quickly out, as tall as a flag-pole and as charming as a walking stick; and she stood with her feet at the bottom of the well and her two arms resting upon the top; and Drakesbill climbed nimbly on her back, and hip! hop! hup! how soon he was up and singing louder than ever, "Quack, quack, quack, when shall I get my money back?"

The King, who was still at the table, heard him singing, and the song made him so angry that he almost choked.

"Can't anybody make that fellow hush?" he cried.

Then he ordered his men to build a great fire, and, when it was hot, to throw Drakesbill into it and burn him up for a wicked wizard.

But Drakesbill was not much afraid this time; he remembered his sweetheart River. Just when the flames were the highest, and the captain of the King's men was going to toss him into them, he sang out:—

> "River, River, outward flow,
> Or into the fire I must go!"

Then friend River, who had only been waiting for these words, flowed quickly out, as strong as a storm and as swift as the wind; and she put out the fire, and drowned all the people that had kindled it; and, glou! glou! glou! she flowed into the King's palace and stood four feet deep in the great hall. And Drakesbill, spruce and fresh as ever, swam hither and thither, singing, "Quack, quack, quack, when shall I get my money back?"

Of course, after all this had happened, the King was more angry than he had ever been before; and when he saw Drakesbill swimming about so coolly, while he had to stand on the table to keep his feet dry, he could hardly hold himself.

"Bring the fellow here, and I'll finish him with the carving knife! bring him here quick!" he cried.

Two servants rushed out and seized Drakesbill very rudely. They dragged him towards the King, who was standing with drawn carving knife. The King's brave men with swords in their hands were all around him. "It is all over with me now," said Drakesbill. "I don't see how I can live through this!"

But just then he thought of his neighbor Wasp-nest, and he cried out:—

> "Wasp-nest, Wasp-nest, hither fly,
> Or Drakesbill soon will have to die!"

Then Wasp-nest, who had been waiting for these words, began to wake up his wasps, and things changed very quickly.

"Buzz, buzz, buzz! Charge!" cried Wasp-nest. And the wasps rushed out and threw themselves upon the King and his brave men, and stung them so badly that they ran and jumped right out from the windows, and nobody in the palace ever saw them again.

As for Drakesbill, he could only sit still and wonder what was going to happen next. But after awhile he remembered his money, and began to sing as before. Then, as the house was very still, he thought that he might as well look round a little while; perhaps he would find his hundred yellow pieces of gold.

It was of no use, however. He peeped into all the corners and opened all the drawers. There was not a dollar in the house. The King had spent everything.

By and by Drakesbill found his way into the room where the King's throne stood, and as he was very tired, he sat down to rest among the cushions of velvet and gold.

When the people saw the King and his brave men running away from the wasps, they felt sure that they would never come back. So they crowded into the palace to see what was the matter. And the only person they found there was little Drakesbill sitting by himself on the throne. Then they all shouted:—

> "The King is dead! long live the King!
> How glad we'll be to be ruled by this thing!"

And one of them ran and fetched the golden crown; and they put it on Drakesbill's head and hailed him as king. And Drakesbill, who had made up his mind not to be surprised at anything, sat very still and took it all as a matter of course.

"He doesn't look much like a king," whispered a few idle fellows; but they were soon driven out of the hall and made to understand that it was wrong even to think such words.

"He will be the best king we have ever had," said others. And some who had known him before said: "A Drakesbill is better any day than a king who does nothing but spend our money."

And that is the way in which little Drakesbill became king. When he had been crowned, and the people had finished shouting, he made a speech from the throne. "Ladies and gentlemen," he said, "I am very hungry. Let us all go to supper."

Lesson 7

The Golden Rule (Do unto others as you would have them do unto you) applies to the way we treat another person's property.

Activity: Let your children pick an item that belongs to Mom or Dad (with your guidance as to age appropriateness) and "borrow" it for a day. Make a contract and have them sign it and talk about how they must take care of the item. The contract could include the condition in which you expect it to be returned and the time limit for borrowing.

Lesson 8

Finish up with any other discussion, ideas, or celebration your family enjoys. Keep up this habit while going forth to concentrate on a new one.

Have a Parent Share moment to share a story from your life or tell about a person who exemplifies this habit.

Obedience

Submitting to the restraint or command of authority

Parent Prep

Read detailed thoughts about Obedience on pages 96–101 of *Laying Down the Rails* and skim the lessons below.

♦ Goals for this Habit (and steps to get there)

_____

_____

_____

♦ A Person or Story from My Life that Demonstrates this Habit

_____

_____

_____

♦ Additional Stories, Poems, Quotations, Bible Verses I Want to Use

_____

_____

_____

♦ Other Activities We Could Do to Practice this Habit

_____

_____

_____

_____

♦ Celebration Ideas

_____

_____

_____

The habit of Obedience is one of the "Top Three" habits that Charlotte talked about most. The other two are Attention and Truthfulness.

Some of these habits, like Obedience, can and should begin during the baby years.

For Obedience, there are more points for parents to practice than there are for children. Parents may want to have their own extra training time to help themselves get in the habit of teaching Obedience.

📖 *1. Make obedience a top priority, even more important than academics.*

Lesson 1

Read the definition and discuss Obedience. Share with the children any goals you've identified for this habit (for instance, "It is expected that obedience will occur the first time a command is spoken."). Also get their input on changes they think need to be made.

Read the Biblical principle found in Ephesians 6:1–3 from your preferred version of the Bible. Children are directly spoken to in this passage and are commanded to obey their parents.

Notes

Before you read the poem, make sure the children know what a parasol is. They will better be able to picture the poem in their minds if they have the correct context.

 3. Realize that you are on assignment from God to teach your child obedience.

4. Remember that your ultimate goal is a child who desires to obey.

5. Expect obedience and convey that expectation in a quiet, but firm, tone of voice.

6. Insist on prompt, cheerful, and lasting obedience every time.

7. Never give a command that you do not intend to see carried out to the full.

8. Be careful of giving so many commands that your child feels pestered.

 9. Teach your child to appeal respectfully; be gracious enough to yield sometimes in matters that are not crucial.

 Habit points from Laying Down the Rails

Lesson 2

Discuss point two. Talk about the temptations of Jesus and how the Devil tempted Him not with overt sins, but with acts of willfulness (Matthew 4:1–11). Read the poem, "Naughty Nelly and Her New Parasol," as an example in a child's life.

2. Willfulness can be the same thing as disobedience.

Naughty Nelly and Her New Parasol
from *The Infant's Delight*

"No, Nelly! not today, my child!
   I cannot let you take it;
This cold March wind, so strong and wild,
   Your parasol, 'twould break it!"

So said Mamma; but Nelly thought,
   "I will take my new present:
'Tis mine; to please me it was bought;
   The weather's bright and pleasant."
So naughty Nelly slyly took
   What kind Mamma had bought her,
And out she went—and, only look!
   The wild March wind has caught her!

The silk tore up, the ribs broke out,
   In spite of Nelly's swaying;
And people laughed at her, no doubt—
   That comes of disobeying.

Lesson 3

Discuss point nine with everyone, suggesting scenarios in which this point might be used correctly. Discuss the quotation that follows, if desired.

9. Appeal respectfully to your parents when you feel strongly that you have right on your side.

"The word no carries a lot more meaning when spoken by a parent who also knows how to say yes." — Joyce Maynard

Activity: Play a game such as Red Light, Green Light; Simon Says; or Mother, May I, in which children obey your "instructions."

Lesson 4

Talk over point eleven.

11. The child who learns to make himself do what he should (even when he doesn't feel like it) will be able to accomplish much in this life.

Read Deuteronomy chapter 30. God has always placed a high priority on obedience. He assured Israel that blessings would come if they obeyed Him. Even after disobedience, if they returned, He would restore blessing. First John 5:1–5 tells us that our love of God is shown by obedience to His commands. We love Him by obeying Him.

 10. Begin teaching obedience by the time your child is one year old.

Lesson 5

Discuss point twelve. Young children are under the protection of their parents' authority because they often cannot discern right from wrong, wise from unwise.

 12. Respond to your conscience, but do not depend on it solely.

Activity: Give a command or two to be carried out by each child within a short time limit. Example: "Get a mug out of the cabinet, fill it with water, heat it up in the microwave for 1 minute." Practice speaking in a positive, firm voice, and let your child practice cheerful, prompt obedience. Make sure the commands are useful and respect the child as a person. For example, don't ask anyone to do silly commands just to prove your authority (like "Put all the magazines in the bathtub" then "Take all the magazines out of the bathtub"). Those types of Obedience drills seem disrespectful to the child as a person.

 13. Give reasons for your commands when appropriate and helpful, but don't feel trapped into doing so every time.

Lesson 6

Discuss point fifteen. Share examples of how discipline brings freedom. The more you obey your parents and other authorities, the more they can trust you to do what's right. The more they trust you to do what's right, the more freedom they can grant you.

 14. Whenever possible, plan ahead to make transitions smooth by giving your child a predetermined amount of time to prepare for the change in activity.

 15. Discipline brings freedom, and obedience is both delightful and dignified.

Read 2 Kings 5:1-16. Naaman was insulted when he was told to wash in the muddy Jordan River to rid his body of leprosy. His companions talked him into obeying the commands of Elisha and he received healing. His obedience brought freedom from his disease, but he almost missed that freedom by not obeying Elisha's command.

Lesson 7

Talk about point sixteen. At some point in time, children will leave home and no longer be under parental authority. It will be very important that they understand they are still under the authority of government, church, employer, and God. There will always be someone over them (and likely others under them), and it will serve them best to accept their position without constant kicking against the goads. Read and discuss "Dr. Johnson and His Father."

 16. The ultimate goal in obedience training is for you to choose to obey all authority.

Dr. Johnson and His Father
from *Thirty More Famous Stories Retold* by James Baldwin

Scene First

It is in a little bookshop in the city of Lichfield, England. The floor has just been swept and the shutter taken down from the one small window. The hour is early, and customers have not yet begun to drop in. Out of doors the rain is falling.

At a small table near the door, a feeble, white-haired old man is making up some packages of books. As he arranges them in a large basket, he stops now and then as though disturbed by pain. He puts his hand to his side; he coughs in a most distressing way; then he sits down and rests himself, leaning his elbows upon the table.

"Samuel!" he calls.

In the farther corner of the room there is a young man busily reading from a large book that is spread open before him. He is a very odd-looking fellow, perhaps eighteen years of age, but you would take him to be older. He is large and awkward, with a great round face, scarred and marked by a strange disease. His eyesight must be poor, for, as he reads, he bends down until his face is quite near the printed page.

"Samuel!" again the old man calls.

But Samuel makes no reply. He is so deeply interested in his book that he does not hear. The old man rests himself a little longer and then finishes tying his packages. He lifts the heavy basket and sets it on the table. The exertion brings on another fit of coughing; and when it is over he calls for the third time, "Samuel!"

"What is it, father?" This time the call is heard.

"You know, Samuel," he says, "that tomorrow is market day at Uttoxeter, and our stall must be attended to. Some of our friends will be there to look at the new books which they expect me to bring. One of us must go down on the stage this morning and get everything in readiness. But I hardly feel able for the journey. My cough troubles me quite a little, and you see that it is raining very hard."

"Yes, father; I am sorry," answers Samuel; and his face is again bent over the book.

"I thought perhaps you would go down to the market, and that I might stay here at the shop," says his father. But Samuel does not hear. He is deep in the study of some Latin classic.

The old man goes to the door and looks out. The rain is still falling. He shivers, and buttons his coat.

It is a twenty-mile ride to Uttoxeter. In five minutes the stage will pass the door.

"Samuel, will you not go down to the market for me this time?"

The old man is putting on his great coat.

He is reaching for his hat.

The basket is on his arm.

He casts a beseeching glance at his son, hoping that he will relent at the last moment.

"Here comes the coach, Samuel;" and the old man is choked by another fit of coughing.

Whether Samuel hears or not, I do not know. He is still reading, and he makes no sign nor motion.

The stage comes rattling down the street.

The old man with his basket of books staggers out of the door. The stage halts for a moment while he climbs inside. Then the driver swings his whip, and all are away.

Samuel, in the shop, still bends over his book.

Out of doors the rain is falling.

Scene Second

Just fifty years have passed, and again it is market day at Uttoxeter.

The rain is falling in the streets. The people who have wares to sell huddle under the eaves and in the stalls and booths that have roofs above them.

A chaise from Lichfield pulls up at the entrance to the market square.

An old man alights. One would guess him to be seventy years of age. He is large and not well-shaped. His face is seamed and scarred, and he makes strange grimaces as he clambers out of the chaise. He wheezes and puffs as though afflicted with asthma. He walks with the aid of a heavy stick.

With slow but ponderous strides he enters the market place and looks around. He seems not to know that the rain is falling.

He looks at the little stalls ranged along the walls of the market place. Some have roofs over them and are the centers of noisy trade. Others have fallen into disuse and are empty.

The stranger halts before one of the latter. "Yes, this is it," he says. He has a strange habit of talking aloud to himself. "I remember it well. It was here that my father, on certain market days, sold books to the clergy of the county. The good men came from every parish to see his wares and to hear him describe their contents."

He turns abruptly around. "Yes, this is the place," he repeats.

He stands quite still and upright, directly in front of the little old stall. He takes off his hat and holds it beneath his arm. His great walking stick has fallen into the gutter. He bows his head and clasps his hands. He does not seem to know that the rain is falling.

The clock in the tower above the market strikes eleven. The passers-by stop and gaze at the stranger. The market people peer at him from their booths and stalls. Some laugh as the rain runs in streams down his scarred old cheeks. Rain is it? Or can it be tears?

Boys hoot at him. Some of the ruder ones even hint at throwing mud; but a sense of shame withholds them from the act.

"The stranger has stood a whole hour in the market place."

"He is a poor lunatic. Let him alone," say the more compassionate.

The rain falls upon his bare head and his broad shoulders. He is drenched and chilled. But he stands motionless and silent, looking neither to the right nor to the left.

"Who is that old fool?" asks a thoughtless young man who chances to be passing.

"Do you ask who he is?" answers a gentleman from London. "Why, he is Dr. Samuel Johnson, the most famous man in England. It was he who wrote *Rasselas* and the *Lives of the Poets* and *Irene* and many another work which all men are praising. It was he who made the great *English Dictionary*, the most wonderful book of our times. In London, the noblest lords and ladies take pleasure in doing him honor. He is the literary lion of England."

"Then why does he come to Uttoxeter and stand thus in the pouring rain?"

"I cannot tell you; but doubtless he has reasons for doing so;" and the gentleman passes on.

At length there is a lull in the storm. The birds are chirping among the housetops. The people wonder if the rain is over, and venture out into the slippery street.

The clock in the tower above the market strikes twelve. The renowned stranger has stood a whole hour motionless in the market place. And again the rain is falling.

Slowly now he returns his hat to his head. He finds his walking stick where it had fallen. He lifts his eyes reverently for a moment, and then, with a lordly, lumbering

Charlotte wrote directly to young people about Obedience in Volume 4, Book 2, page 145.

motion, walks down the street to meet the chaise which is ready to return to Lichfield.

We follow him through the pattering rain to his native town.

"Why, Dr. Johnson!" exclaims his hostess; "we have missed you all day. And you are so wet and chilled! Where have you been?"

"Madam," says the great man, "fifty years ago, this very day, I tacitly refused to oblige or obey my father. The thought of the pain which I must have caused him has haunted me ever since. To do away the sin of that hour, I this morning went in a chaise to Uttoxeter and did do penance publicly before the stall which my father had formerly used."

The great man bows his head upon his hands and sobs.

Out of doors the rain is falling.

Lesson 8

Read "Over in the Meadow" as an illustration of Obedience, then have a Parent Share moment to share a story from your life or tell about a person who exemplifies Obedience.

Over in the Meadow
by Olive A. Wadsworth

Over in the meadow,
  In the sand in the sun
Lived an old mother toadie
  And her little toadie one.
"Wink!" said the mother;
  "I wink!" said the one,
So they winked and they blinked
  In the sand in the sun.

Over in the meadow,
  Where the stream runs blue
Lived an old mother fish
  And her little fishes two.
"Swim!" said the mother;
  "We swim!" said the two,
So they swam and they leaped
  Where the stream runs blue.

Over in the meadow,
  In a hole in a tree
Lived an old mother bluebird
  And her little birdies three.
"Sing!" said the mother;
  "We sing!" said the three,
So they sang and were glad
  In a hole in the tree.

Over in the meadow,
  In the reeds on the shore
Lived an old mother muskrat

And her little ratties four.
"Dive!" said the mother;
  "We dive!" said the four,
So they dived and they burrowed
  In the reeds on the shore.

Over in the meadow,
  In a snug beehive
Lived a mother honey bee
  And her little bees five.
"Buzz!" said the mother;
  "We buzz!" said the five,
So they buzzed and they hummed
  In the snug beehive.

Over in the meadow,
  In a nest built of sticks
Lived a black mother crow
  And her little crows six.
"Caw!" said the mother;
  "We caw!" said the six,
So they cawed and they called
  In their nest built of sticks.

Over in the meadow,
  Where the grass is so even
Lived a gay mother cricket
  And her little crickets seven.
"Chirp!" said the mother;
  "We chirp!" said the seven,
So they chirped cheery notes
  In the grass soft and even.

Over in the meadow,
  By the old mossy gate
Lived a brown mother lizard
  And her little lizards eight.
"Bask!" said the mother;
  "We bask!" said the eight,
So they basked in the sun
  On the old mossy gate.

Over in the meadow,
  Where the quiet pools shine
Lived a green mother frog
  And her little froggies nine.
"Croak!" said the mother;
  "We croak!" said the nine,
So they croaked and they splashed
  Where the quiet pools shine.

Over in the meadow,
In a sly little den
Lived a gray mother spider
And her little spiders ten.
"Spin!" said the mother;
"We spin!" said the ten,
So they spun lacy webs
In their sly little den.

Lesson 9

The Ten Commandments are well known and easily remembered. If you wish, the family can spend some time memorizing them as you continue Obedience habit training.

Read the Ten Commandments in Exodus 20:1–17. From the earliest days of man, God has given commands and the responsibility to obey those commands.

Lesson 10

Demonstrate how Obedience is partly for the child's protection. You could use the example of a parent's yelling, "Stop!" as a child is about to run into a busy street.

Activity: Blindfold one of the children and lead him or her through an obstacle course using only your instructions. The child must listen carefully and obey in order not to run into any of the obstacles. You could use toys on the floor or chairs and boxes or you could move the furniture slightly so that it is in unexpected locations.

Lesson 11

Discuss how the following passages of Scripture relate to Obedience.

Proverbs 15:5—Obedience to instruction is wise.
Proverbs 15:31–33—Ignoring discipline and instruction shows contempt for yourself.
Romans 13:1–7—We should submit to governing authorities.
Hebrews 13:17—Obedience causes joy instead of a burden.

Lesson 12

Obedience is a foundational habit and will take a lot of practice. If you want to continue habit training in obedience, spend several weeks reading the following Bible stories, one at a time, and have your children explain the place of obedience in each story.

1 Samuel 15—King Saul disobeyed God.
Luke 2:41–52—Jesus obeyed His parents.
Mark 6:34–56—The disciples obeyed Jesus though they didn't understand what He planned to do.
Acts 9:1–22—Ananias obeyed God's direction though he may have been afraid of Saul.

Finish up with any other discussion, ideas, or celebration your family enjoys. Keep up this habit while going forth to concentrate on a new one.

Personal Initiative

Acting at one's own discretion, independently of outside influence or control

Parent Prep

Read detailed thoughts about Personal Initiative on pages 101–103 of *Laying Down the Rails* and skim the lessons below.

♦ Goals for this Habit (and steps to get there)

_____

_____

_____

♦ A Person or Story from My Life that Demonstrates this Habit

_____

_____

_____

♦ Additional Stories, Poems, Quotations, Bible Verses I Want to Use

_____

_____

_____

♦ Other Activities We Could Do to Practice this Habit

_____

_____

_____

♦ Celebration Ideas

_____

_____

_____

Lesson 1

Read the definition and discuss Personal Initiative. Share with the children any goals you've identified for this habit (for instance, "Experimenting and pursuing interests will be encouraged."). Also get their input on changes they think need to be made.

Read the Biblical principle found in 1 John 3:16–18 from your preferred version of the Bible. As Christians, our faith should result in our taking initiative to help those in need.

📖 *1. Make sure your child has plenty of free time to play, explore, and grow.*

📖 *2. Be available to guide, inform, and give direction as needed.*

📖 *3. Don't sacrifice the habit of personal initiative because you are uptight about controlling all the other habits you want to cultivate in your child.*

📖 *5. Allow your child freedom to express his personality in his school work within the boundaries you have set.*

📖 Habit points from *Laying Down the Rails*

Lesson 2

Discuss point four together. It takes effort, but learning to entertain yourself gets easier the more you do it.

 4. **Invent your own games and find things to do within the boundaries set by your parents.**

Activity: Let the children think of an activity that illustrates Personal Initiative. Or let them invent a game that they would enjoy playing with their friends.

Lesson 3

It is freeing to find that we do not have to depend on others to entertain us, get us a drink of water, find our lost possessions, and so on. Read and discuss "Five Little Chickens."

Five Little Chickens
Author Unknown

Said the first little chicken,
With a strange little squirm,
"I wish I could find
A fat little worm."

Said the next little chicken,
With an odd little shrug,
"I wish I could find
A fat little bug."

Said a third little chicken,
With a small sigh of grief,
"I wish I could find
A green little leaf!"

Said the fourth little chicken,
With a faint little moan,
"I wish I could find
A wee gravel stone."

"Now, see here!" said the mother,
From the green garden patch,
"If you want any breakfast,
Just come here and scratch!"

Lesson 4

There will be many times when someone needs to step up and lead a job to completion or maybe save a group from stupidity.

Read 1 Samuel 25:1–42. Abigail acted wisely in place of her husband's foolishness and saved her household from David and his band of men. She also saved David from vengeful bloodshed.

Lesson 5

Read and discuss "The Stone in the Road." Don't leave a job undone for lack of supervision or thinking that somebody else will take care of it.

The Stone in the Road
from *Harper's Third Reader*, edited by James Baldwin

A long time ago there lived a king who took great delight in teaching his people good habits.

"Bad luck comes only to the lazy and the careless," said he; "but to the busy workers God gives the good things of this life."

One night he put a large stone in the middle of the road near his palace, and then watched to see what the people who passed that way would do.

Early in the morning a sturdy old farmer, named Peter came along with his heavy ox-cart loaded with corn.

"Oh, these lazy people!" he cried, driving his oxen to one side of the road. "Here is this big stone right in the middle of the road, and nobody will take the trouble to move it!"

And he went on his way, scolding about the laziness of other people, but never thinking of touching the stone himself.

Then there came a young soldier, singing a merry song as he walked along. A gay feather was stuck in his hat and a big sword hung at his side; and he was fond of telling great stories of what he had done in the war. He held his head so high that he did not see the stone, but stumbled over it and fell flat in the dust.

This put an end to his merry song; and as he rose to his feet he began to storm at the country people.

"Silly drones!" he said, "to have no more sense than to leave a stone like that in the middle of the road!"

Then he passed on; but he did not sing anymore.

An hour later there came down the road six merchants with their goods on pack horses, going to the fair that was to be held near the village. When they reached the stone the road was so narrow that they could hardly drive their horses between it and the wall.

"Did anyone ever see the like?" they said. "There is that big stone in the road, and not a man in all the country but that is too lazy to move it!"

And so the stone lay there for three weeks; it was in everybody's way, and yet everybody left it for somebody else to move. Then the king sent word to all his people to meet together on a certain day near his palace, as he had something to tell them.

The day came, and a great crowd of men and women gathered in the road. Old Peter, the farmer, was there, and so were the merchants and the young soldier.

"I hope that the king will now find out what a lazy set of people he has around him," said Peter.

And then the sound of a horn was heard, and the king was seen coming towards them. He rode up to the stone, got down from his horse, and said:

"My friends, it was I who put this stone here, three weeks ago. It has been seen by everyone of you; and yet everyone has left it just where it was, and has scolded his neighbor for not moving it out of the way."

Then he stooped down and rolled the stone over. Underneath the stone was a round hollow place, in which was a small iron box. The king held up the box so that all the people might see what was written on a piece of paper fastened to it.

These were the words:

"For him who lifts the stone."

He opened the box, turned it upside down, and out of it fell a beautiful gold ring and twenty bright gold coins.

Then everyone wished that he had only thought of moving the stone instead of going around it and finding fault with his neighbor. There are very many people still who lose prizes because they think it easier to find fault than to do the work which lies before them. Such people do not usually blame themselves, but think it is all on account of bad luck and hard times.

Lesson 6

Read and discuss the quotation below. Helen Keller included this statement when talking about the illusion of security. Security is never guaranteed. One should be prudent but not paranoid. We shouldn't allow worry or anxiety to quench Personal Initiative. Read and enjoy the poem that follows.

"Life is either a daring adventure, or nothing." — *Helen Keller*

The Road Not Taken
by Robert Frost

Two roads diverged in a yellow wood,
And sorry I could not travel both
And be one traveler, long I stood
And looked down one as far as I could
To where it bent in the undergrowth;

Then took the other, as just as fair,
And having perhaps the better claim,
Because it was grassy and wanted wear;
Though as for that the passing there
Had worn them really about the same,

And both that morning equally lay
In leaves no step had trodden black.
Oh, I kept the first for another day!
Yet knowing how way leads on to way,
I doubted if I should ever come back.

I shall be telling this with a sigh
Somewhere ages and ages hence:
Two roads diverged in a wood, and I—
I took the one less traveled by,
And that has made all the difference.

Lesson 7

Read and discuss the quotation below.

"You cannot build character and courage by taking away man's initiative and independence." — Abraham Lincoln

Activity: Let your child think of an activity that he would really like to try. Maybe it's one he has mentioned before but you always put it off because it is too messy, or maybe you have always taken the lead in the project in such a way that the child barely participated. It could be a science experiment, baking, making a meal, or simply digging in the dirt. Allow each child to try his interest on his own if he is capable. Teach some helpful hints first to minimize the mess. Tell the children that they are in charge, and they can even tell you what to do if they want your help. Let them fail if that is the direction you see them headed. Encourage them. Let them lead in clean-up time as well.

Lesson 8

Jesus was not afraid to make a scene if the situation called for it. He was not afraid of doing what was right, knowing that someone might be offended.

Read Luke 13:10–17. Jesus noticed a crippled woman while He was teaching in the synagogue, called her forth, and healed her in front of everyone. The grouchy synagogue ruler made a scene about it, so Jesus jumped right in to rebuke him for embarrassing this poor woman. The people were delighted.

Lesson 9

Deciding on the right course of action can be tricky. You might not get it right at first. But then again, you just might. Read and discuss "Out of the Woods."

Out of the Woods
from *Harper's Third Reader*, edited by James Baldwin

Part I

In a rocky part of the state of New York there once lived a poor widow and her little girl, a brown-eyed child of seven, named Alice. The cold weather was coming. The frost had already withered the grass in the meadows, and turned the green of the maple leaves into bright gold and scarlet. Yes, cold weather was near at hand; and winter is no good friend to the poor.

"Well, Alice," said her mother one morning, "we shall certainly not starve this winter, for there are plenty of potatoes in the cellar. But I don't know what we shall have to wear; I cannot buy any new clothes."

"We'll wear our old ones, then," said Alice.

"And they are so thin that we shall have to stay indoors all winter," said her mother. "But luckily there is plenty of wood, and we shall not freeze."

Alice grew very thoughtful, and her brown eyes looked as though they were full of trouble. She had run about all summer as happy as the birds in the leafy woods, and had not thought of the winter. What could she do to help her mother? If something to eat were needed, it would be easy for her to help; she could pick up nuts in the woods— bushels of them. But to find something to wear—that was a great deal harder.

As she sat on the doorstep puzzling her little head about this matter, her eyes happened to fall upon a necklace she had that morning made of scarlet berries, and a queer thought came into her mind: she would make a dress of leaves—of bright red leaves. She fancied that thus she might in some strange manner help her mother. She had a spool of thread and a needle in her pocket. She would run off to the woods without saying anything about it.

Once in the woods, Alice had no trouble in finding leaves enough, bright red ones, too—so red that they made her eyes blink as she held them up towards the sun. She filled her apron with them, and then seated herself on a low stone, ready for work, surrounded like a queen with scarlet and gold. The tiny fingers were very quick and cunning. Leaf after leaf they sewed together until something a little like a dainty dress was shaped, and carefully fitted to the little body.

"Don't I look pretty?" laughed Alice, as she looked down at her leafy skirt. "But I must make a new hat, too. It would not do to wear my old sunbonnet with such a handsome dress."

Again the thread and needle were set to work, and soon a queer looking cap, placed jauntily on her head, made the child look like a little fairy of the woods.

She picked her way carefully through the wood, intending to run home and show her fine, new suit to her troubled mother. But when she reached the opening, she stopped, fixed to the spot with wonder. A strange man was before her, sitting on a crooked bench, and doing something to a big board fastened to three long sticks in front of him.

The stranger seemed as much surprised as Alice; but, as she was about to run back into the wood, he called out, "Who in the world are you, little fairy, and who dressed you up in that way?"

He looked so pleasant that Alice could not help giving him a laugh for his smile, as she answered: "I am Alice, and I did it all myself. Isn't it pretty?"

"Yes, indeed; and what made you think of such a dress?"

Then Alice told him all about it—how poor they were that year, and how troubled her mother was; in fact, she chattered away until she had told all her small history, some parts of which made the stranger's face look sad, while others made him smile.

"And now," said he, when she had finished, "do you think you could stand still for a short time?"

Alice at once became motionless, and the stranger began to work away at the big board before him. In a little while he said, "There, you may move now; sit down on that stone and rest." Then Alice sat down until he asked if she felt like standing again, when she sprang to her feet and stood as before. She was beginning to feel very tired when he said, "That will do, little one; come, and look at this."

Part II

Alice went and stood by the side of the stranger. What was it that she saw on the board before them? It was her own self—scarlet dress and all—her black curls clustering about her head, her big brown eyes wide open, and her cheeks as pink as the sunset clouds.

"Why, that's me!" she cried.

"Of course it is," laughed the stranger.

"But I wish I had my shoes on. I have a pair at the house, but I only wear them in the winter."

"The picture is prettier as it is," said the artist.

Then, taking something like a piece of green paper from his pocket, he put it in her hand, saying, "Give this to your mother and tell her to buy you a nice warm dress with it. I am coming to see you tomorrow; and now, good-bye, little maid!"

He stooped down and kissed her, and Alice, covered with red leaves and holding the green leaf in her hand, ran away up the hillside. She rushed into the house, and astonished her mother, not so much by her strange appearance as by the wonderful story which she told.

"I wonder who the man is," said the mother. "Three sticks—a big board—he must be an artist." Then her eyes fell upon the green piece of paper. "Why, child!" she cried, "he has given you ten dollars!"

"Ten dollars!" cried Alice. She had not seen so much money for many a day.

The next morning the stranger called at the house, and explained it all. He showed them how the big board and the three sticks were used; and Alice stood before him again in her dress of autumn leaves.

For many mornings after that the artist came back to the woodland cottage, always to paint Alice's picture; and every time he became more and more interested in the bright little child. As for Alice, she opened her eyes with wonder, when she was told that her picture was to be taken to New York to hang "in a big room called the Academy."

At length the stranger bade them good-by, and went back to the city. Alice spent the long winter months very merrily in her mother's lonely cottage; for the money which the artist had given her had bought plenty of warm clothing, and her mother's face was no longer sad.

At last winter gave place to spring; and on the walls of the Academy in the great city hung the picture of a bright-faced little girl, clad and capped with scarlet leaves, coming out of the dim, gray woods. Of all the visitors there, not one passed it by—all stopped to admire the brown-eyed child so quaintly clad. In the end a rich man bought the picture for the sake of saying that "the gem of the Academy" was his own.

One fine May day a letter came to Alice and her mother. It was from the artist, and within it was a check for fifty dollars for "the little fairy of the woods." And this was but the beginning of brighter days and a happier fortune—all of which resulted from Alice's dressmaking in the autumn woods.

Lesson 10

Discuss the Thomas Jefferson quotation below.

"It is wonderful how much may be done if we are always doing." — Thomas Jefferson

Have a Parent Share moment to share a story from your life or tell about a person who exemplifies Personal Initiative.

Lesson 11

Read and discuss "The Cup of Water," then finish up with any other discussion, ideas, or celebration your family enjoys. Keep up this habit while going forth to concentrate on a new one.

The Cup of Water
adapted from *A Book of Golden Deeds* by Charlotte M. Yonge

No touch in the history of the minstrel king David gives us a more warm and personal feeling towards him than his longing for the water of the well of Bethlehem. Standing as the incident does in the summary of the characters of his mighty men, it is apt to appear to us as if it had taken place in his latter days; but such is not the case, it befell while he was still under thirty, in the time of his persecution by Saul.

It was when the last attempt at reconciliation with the king had been made, when the affectionate parting with the generous and faithful Jonathan had taken place, when Saul was hunting him like a partridge on the mountains on the one side, and the Philistines had nearly taken his life on the other, that David, outlawed, yet loyal at the heart, sent his aged parents to the land of Moab for refuge, and himself took up his abode in the caves of the wild limestone hills that had become familiar to him when he was a shepherd. Brave captain and Heaven-destined king as he was, his name attracted around him a motley group of those that were in distress, or in debt, or discontented, and among them were the 'mighty men' whose brave deeds won them the foremost parts in that army with which David was to fulfill the ancient promises to his people. There were his three nephews, Joab, the ferocious and imperious, the chivalrous Abishai, and Asahel the fleet of foot; there was the warlike Levite Benaiah, who slew lions and lionlike men, and others who, like David himself, had done battle with the gigantic sons of Anak. Yet even these valiant men, so wild and lawless, could be kept in check by the voice of their young captain; and, outlaws as they were, they spoiled no peaceful villages, they lifted not their hands against the persecuting monarch, and the neighboring farms lost not one lamb through their violence. Some at least listened to the song of their warlike minstrel:

'Come, ye children, and hearken to me,
I will teach you the fear of the Lord.
What man is he that lusteth to live,
And would fain see good days?
Let him refrain his tongue from evil
And his lips that they speak no guile,
Let him eschew evil and do good,
Let him seek peace and ensue it.'

With such strains as these, sung to his harp, the warrior gained the hearts of his men to enthusiastic love, and gathered followers on all sides, among them eleven fierce men of Gad, with faces like lions and feet swift as roes, who swam the Jordan in time of flood, and fought their way to him, putting all enemies in the valleys to flight.

But the Eastern sun burnt on the bare rocks. A huge fissure, opening in the mountain ridge, encumbered at the bottom with broken rocks, with precipitous banks, scarcely affording a foothold for the wild goats—such is the spot where, upon a cleft on the steep precipice, still remain the foundations of the 'hold', or tower, believed to have been David's retreat, and near at hand is the low-browed entrance of the galleried cave alternating between narrow passages and spacious halls, but all oppressively hot and close. Waste and wild, without a bush or a tree, in the feverish atmosphere of Palestine, it was a desolate region, and at length the wanderer's heart fainted in him, as he thought of his own home, with its rich and lovely terraced slopes, green with wheat, trellised with vines, and clouded with grey olive, and of the cool cisterns of living water by the gate of which he loved to sing—

'He shall feed me in a green pasture,
And lead me forth beside the waters of comfort'.

His parched longing lips gave utterance to the sigh, 'Oh that one would give me to drink of the water of the well of Bethlehem that is by the gate?'

Three of his brave men, apparently Abishai, Benaiah, and Eleazar, heard the wish. Between their mountain fastness and the dearly loved spring lay the host of the Philistines; but their love for their leader feared no enemies. It was not only water that he longed for, but the water from the fountain which he had loved in his childhood.

They descended from their chasm, broke through the midst of the enemy's army, and drew the water from the favorite spring, bearing it back, once again through the foe, to the tower upon the rock! Deeply moved was their chief at this act of self-devotion—so much moved that the water seemed to him to be too sacred to be put to his own use. 'May God forbid it me that I should do this thing. Shall I drink the blood of these men that have put their lives in jeopardy, for with the jeopardy of their lives they brought it?' And as a hallowed and precious gift, he poured out unto the Lord the water obtained at the price of such peril to his followers.

Reverence

Consideration for others; respect for person and property

Parent Prep

Read detailed thoughts about Reverence on pages 103–105 of *Laying Down the Rails* and skim the lessons below.

♦ Goals for this Habit (and steps to get there)

_____

_____

_____

♦ A Person or Story from My Life that Demonstrates this Habit

_____

_____

_____

♦ Additional Stories, Poems, Quotations, Bible Verses I Want to Use

_____

_____

_____

♦ Other Activities We Could Do to Practice this Habit

_____

_____

_____

♦ Celebration Ideas

_____

_____

_____

1. Be prepared to exert a lot of zeal and persistence to cultivate within your child a respect for others.

Lesson 1

Read the definition and discuss Reverence. Share with the children any goals you've identified for this habit (for instance, "We will treat our siblings as we would treat our best friends."). Also get their input on changes they think need to be made.

Read the Biblical principle found in Romans 12:10 and 16 from your preferred version of the Bible. Put others above yourself, no matter if they are an enemy or a nuisance.

Lesson 2

Discuss point two.

 2. Form a sense of respect for historical events and people as well.

Activity: Visit a museum or historic site. Prepare your children beforehand by reading to yourself on the significant things that will be seen or the events that took place. Share interesting information in short snippets or a short talk. Short lessons will encourage Reverence with a good attitude. Talk reverently about the people of the past, relating them to current events or people that you know. Discuss proper behavior that is expected at the site or museum. Make sure the experience is on par with your children's ages and attention spans.

Adjust these activities if they seem too old or too young for your children. Use them as a springboard for your own ideas.

3. Use educational methods that respect your child as a person.

Lesson 3

Every one of us shows some prejudice or rage toward others at times. It may be reserved for the worst criminals, but it is still there. It takes extra grace to see the human side of those who deserve scorn. Read an example of this in "The Little Mother."

The Little Mother
adapted from *An American Book of Golden Deeds* by James Baldwin

They call her the Little Mother—this woman of whom I am telling you. Why they gave her that name will appear as my story proceeds.

The Little Mother devotes much of her time to the doing of golden deeds among those who are commonly supposed to be undeserving of kindness.

She is the friend of wrongdoers, although not of wrongdoing.

You ask how this can be? I will tell you.

In the state prisons of our country, like that of Sing-Sing in New York, there are many men who are undergoing punishment for crimes committed against their fellow-men.

Some of these are hardened criminals without friendships and without friends—men whose lives have been given to wrongdoing.

Some are men who were once respectable and are now suffering punishment for, perhaps, their first offenses against the laws.

Some have wives and children, mothers, sisters, or other loved ones struggling in poverty and disgrace, and with many misgivings hoping darkly for the day of their release.

The most of these men will sooner or later have served out their terms of punishment. They will be given their freedom. They will go out again into the warm sunlight and the wholesome air and the fellowship of their kind.

What will they do then?

Has their punishment made better men of them?

Too often it has not. Too often it has only filled their minds with an ever increasing bitterness towards all the rest of mankind. Too often it has shut the door of hope, and closed the hearts of these men to every kindly influence. Too often it has made them worse instead of better.

And what of the few who go out earnestly wishing to live honest lives and do right?

Do good men offer them a helping hand? Do friends encourage them? Or are they not shunned, mistrusted, shut out from every worthy endeavor?

Habit points from Laying Down the Rails

Can we wonder, therefore, that only a small number of men who have once been in prison ever become good citizens again? Can we wonder that so many are never reformed but return at once to their evil practices?

A hundred and fifty years ago, John Howard, a great and good Englishman, devoted his life to the befriending of prisoners and the improvement of prisons in Europe. A hundred years ago, Elizabeth Fry, a sweet-faced Quakeress, visited the jails of Great Britain and wrought many a golden deed in behalf of the wretched men who were confined in them.

All prisons the world over are today far less horrible than they were in the days of John Howard and Elizabeth Fry.

But the problem of what shall become of the criminal after he has suffered his punishment is perhaps greater now than it ever was before.

It is the problem which came into the mind of the Little Mother one Sunday morning when for the first time she saw the inside of a state prison.

It was in the penitentiary at San Quentin, California. The prisoners were in the chapel. Their faces, "plainly bearing the marring imprint of sorrow and sin," were turned toward her. They were impatiently waiting for such words as she might speak to them, yet hoping for no comfort.

It was the first time that she had seen the prison stripes. It was the first time that she had heard the iron gates; the first time that she had realized the hopelessness of the prisoner's life.

From that day she was resolved to be the friend of the friendless, yes, the friend of even those who have forfeited the right to friendship.

"The touch of human sympathy—that is what every man needs in order to bring out the best that is in him. No man was ever so hopelessly bad that there was not somewhere in his mind or heart some little spark of goodness that might be touched by true sympathy truly expressed."

So argued the Little Mother. She therefore organized a prison league or society for mutual help, and she invited prisoners everywhere to become members of it.

Each member of the league promised to do a few simple things faithfully, as God gave him strength:—

To pray every morning and night.

To refrain from bad language.

To obey the prison rules cheerfully and try to be an example of good conduct.

To cheer and encourage others in well-doing and right living.

Then he was given a little badge to wear on his coat—a white button bearing the motto of the league: LOOK UP AND HOPE. And as soon as the league in any prison numbered several members they were given a little white flag to float above them as they sat in the chapel on Sunday mornings.

All this was very simple. It did not seem to be much, and yet it worked wonders.

It united the men in a bond of brotherhood. It gave them a definite and noble object to strive for. Above all, it told them that they had one friend who was earnestly striving to do them good.

And they united in lovingly calling that one friend their LITTLE MOTHER.

They talked with her about their aims and hopes. They were like children going to their mother for counsel and encouragement.

And they wrote her letters such as this:—

"Little Mother: As I entered the chapel Sunday and looked at our white flag, I thought again of the promises I had made, of all they ought to mean, and I promised God that with his help I would never disgrace it. No one shall see anything in my life that will bring dishonor or stain to its whiteness."

The field of the Little Mother's work widened. From the great prisons in all parts of the country came the call. Would she not visit and talk with the prisoners? Would she not organize a prison league among them?

It was surprising how many of them really and earnestly wished to be better men. The touch of human sympathy—that was what was needed.

And so the Little Mother's golden deeds multiplied. She became known as the prisoners' friend, and hundreds of prisoners vowed to be faithful to her.

Men served their terms of punishment and went home, changed in heart and in purpose. They might meet with scorn, with cruel rebuffs, with cold neglect. But the Little Mother had taught them how to be brave; she would help them to be strong. Every member of the league learned to look up to her; and his conduct after gaining his freedom was made her personal care.

Then through the aid of benevolent men, of prison officers, and of the prisoners themselves, she founded homes in which those who were newly liberated could find shelter until they were able to support themselves by honest labor.

Thus they were prevented from falling into the snares of former evil associates. They were encouraged to persevere in their efforts to attain to a nobler manhood.

These sheltering homes were called Hope Halls. To many a man who otherwise would have despaired and returned to a life of crime, they were the means of salvation.

Thus the Little Mother's golden deeds have produced golden fruit, and hundreds of men have been reclaimed to good citizenship; hundreds of families have been made happy that otherwise would have remained in wretchedness; and the world has been shown that the work of punishment is most efficient when tempered by the touch of human sympathy.

And now shall I tell you the name of this Little Mother? Her name is Maud Ballington Booth. Shall we not say that it is worthy to be placed in the same honor roll with those of Clara Barton, Dorothea Dix, Peter Cooper, and other lovers of humanity?

Lesson 4

Read and discuss the poem below. Respecting your brother or sister is a most important practice and shows what is in your heart. Siblings are the "least of these" in each child's life.

Love Between Brothers and Sisters
by Isaac Watts

Whatever brawls disturb the street,
　　There should be peace at home;
Where sisters dwell and brothers meet,
　　Quarrels should never come.

Birds in their little nests agree;
　　And 'tis a shameful sight,
When children of one family
　　Fall out and chide and fight.

Hard names at first, and threatening words
　　That are but noisy breath,
May grow to clubs and naked swords,
　　To murder and to death.

The devil tempts one mother's son
    To rage against another:
So wicked Cain was hurried on
    'Til he had killed his brother.

The wise will let their anger cool,
    At least before 'tis night;
But in the bosom of a fool
    It burns 'til morning light.

Pardon, O Lord, our childish rage,
    Our little brawls remove;
That, as we grow to riper age,
    Our hearts may all be love.

Lesson 5

Read and discuss the quotation below.

> *"You can easily judge the character of a man by how he treats those who can do nothing for him."* — *Johann Wolfgang von Goethe*

Read Deuteronomy 24:14–22. Foreigners and poor people should be shown compassion and care instead of being taken advantage of. God reminded the Israelites that they were also slaves once.

Lesson 6

Read and discuss the quotation.

> *"There are two types of people—those who come into a room and say, 'Well, here I am!' and those who come in and say, 'Ah, there you are.' "* — *Frederick L. Collins*

Activity: Let the children think of and share ways a person could show consideration for others. You could give scenarios and let them tell you how a person would show Reverence in that situation:

- The local grocer gives out free cookies to the children. The children all want the one with the most sprinkles.
- Everyone has a different opinion when it comes to choosing the story for bedtime.
- One child wants to practice her guitar while another wants to quietly read.
- Two kids go for the same comfy armchair to settle into for family devotions.
- Someone cuts in line in front of you. Do you grumble, tattle, approach them gently, disarm them with a smile and engaging conversation?

Lesson 7

We shouldn't ignore new friends for the sake of old friends; neither should we ignore established friendships in hopes of winning new or better ones. Read and discuss the Aesop fable below.

The Goatherd and the Wild Goats

from *The Aesop for Children* by Milo Winter

One cold stormy day a Goatherd drove his Goats for shelter into a cave, where a number of Wild Goats had also found their way. The Shepherd wanted to make the Wild Goats part of his flock; so he fed them well. But to his own flock, he gave only just enough food to keep them alive. Then the weather cleared, and the Shepherd led the Goats out to feed. The Wild Goats scampered off to the hills.

"Is that the thanks I get for feeding you and treating you so well?" complained the Shepherd.

"Do not expect us to join your flock," replied one of the Wild Goats. "We know how you would treat us later on, if some strangers should come as we did."

It is unwise to treat old friends badly for the sake of new ones.

Feed minds. Inspire hearts. Encourage action.

Lesson 8

James 2:1–7 talks against showing favoritism to the rich at the expense of the poor. Read and discuss the counsel given in the poem below.

Inscription for My Little Son's Silver Plate

by Eugene Field

When thou dost eat from off this plate,
I charge thee be thou temperate;
Unto thine elders at the board
Do thou sweet reverence accord;
And, though to dignity inclined,
Unto the serving-folk be kind;
Be ever mindful of the poor,
Nor turn them hungry from the door;
And unto God, for health and food
And all that in thy life is good,
Give thou thy heart in gratitude.

Lesson 9

Ephesians 5:21 talks about submitting to one another out of reverence for Christ.

Read Nehemiah chapter 5. Some Israelites were taking advantage of their kinsmen and charging great interest on loans of food. Nehemiah told them to stop! Nehemiah himself was not taking the allotment of food the government promised him. (The government had promised it, but the people were the ones who had to pay up.)

Lesson 10

Playing tricks on others often ends in embarrassment and wounds instead of in fun. Read and discuss "The First of April at Hazel Dell."

The First of April at Hazel Dell
from *Harper's Third Reader,* edited by James Baldwin

It was the first day of April, and the boys and girls at the Hazel Dell school had been having a merry time. Tom Brown had pinned a long curled paper to Harry Long's new jacket, and Harry had walked proudly about the playground a long time before he found it out.

Mary Lee had sent Carrie Bell to the front gate to see "a very dear friend;" and the very dear friend was found to be nobody but Franko, the big dog who lived next door. Kitty Clover had told Nellie Hood to "shut her eyes and open her hands for something good," and then had run slyly away, leaving Nellie under the window looking very silly.

"O girls," said Ella Cole, "I am going to play a trick on Margery Hall. You know that her folks are very, very poor, and that she never brings anything for lunch but a slice of bread and butter in a strawberry basket. Well, while she is in the other room, studying her lesson, I am going to take her bread and give it to Franko, and we'll see how funny she'll look when she finds it gone."

"Oh, don't, Ella!" said some of the girls and boys. "She will be hungry, and you will be cruel to throw her dinner away!"

"Do, Ella," said others; "it will be such fun to see her!"

And away went Ella to the closet where the strawberry basket hung under Margery's hat and shawl. In a minute or two she came back with the bread and threw it over the fence to Franko, who ate it at a mouthful.

"Oh, shame!" cried those who had said "Don't!"

But those who had said "Do!" began to laugh; and they laughed louder still when they saw Margery coming out with her basket. And as she lifted the napkin they shouted "April Fool!" But, much to their surprise, the brightest of smiles shone on the child's pale face. And no wonder! The slice of bread was gone, to be sure; but in its place was a nice biscuit, a thick piece of jelly cake, a large orange, and a paper of choice candies.

Then it was that the "Don't" girls and boys, as they saw her take these things out, shouted, "April Fool!" And the "Do" party said never a word, but looked at Ella Cole as if they did not know whether to feel vexed at her or pleased. And hers was the only really pleasant first-of-April joke that I ever heard of.

Lesson 11

Read and discuss the quotation below, then have a Parent Share moment to share a story from your life or tell about a person who exemplifies Reverence.

"It is never too late to give up our prejudices." — *Henry David Thoreau*

Lesson 12

Discuss the connection between the following Scriptures and respect for others.

Proverbs 14:21—Kindness to the needy is blessed.

Proverbs 14:31—Oppression of the poor is contempt toward God; being gracious toward the poor honors God.

Proverbs 17:5—Mocking the poor is contempt toward God.

Proverbs 22:2—Rich and poor have something in common.

Matthew 5:43—6:4—Love your enemies; have right motives when giving to the needy.

Romans 15:1, 2—Build up those who are weak.

Colossians 3:11—All believers are equal in Christ.

Lesson 13

Read and discuss the poem below. Finish up with any other discussion, ideas, or celebration your family enjoys. Keep up this habit while going forth to concentrate on a new one.

The Pedigree of Honey
by Emily Dickinson

The pedigree of honey
Does not concern the bee;
A clover, any time, to him
Is aristocracy.

Self-Control

Keeping back the expression of our passions and emotions

Parent Prep

Read detailed thoughts about Self-Control on pages 105–108 of *Laying Down the Rails* and skim the lessons below.

♦ Goals for this Habit (and steps to get there)

_____

_____

_____

♦ A Person or Story from My Life that Demonstrates this Habit

_____

_____

_____

♦ Additional Stories, Poems, Quotations, Bible Verses I Want to Use

_____

_____

_____

♦ Other Activities We Could Do to Practice this Habit

_____

_____

_____

♦ Celebration Ideas

_____

_____

_____

Lesson 1

Read the definition and discuss Self-Control. Share with the children any goals you've identified for this habit (for instance, "We will count to ten when we feel anger rising."). Also get their input on changes they think need to be made.

Read the Biblical principle found in James 1:19 and 20 from your preferred version of the Bible. This passage is a great synopsis, defining Self-Control.

Lesson 2

Talk about point one, then read and discuss the quotation and the poem.

"The happiness of a man in this life does not consist in the absence but in the mastery of his passions." — *Alfred, Lord Tennyson*

 1. Understand that self-control brings joy.

Anger
by Charles Lamb

Anger in its time and place
May assume a kind of grace.
It must have some reason in it,
And not last beyond a minute.
If to further lengths it go,
It does into malice grow.
'Tis the difference that we see
'Twixt the serpent and the bee.
If the latter you provoke,
It inflicts a hasty stroke,
Puts you to some little pain,
But it *never stings again.*
Close in tufted bush or brake
Lurks the poison-swelled snake
Nursing up his cherished wrath;
In the purlieux of his path,
In the cold, or in the warm,
Mean him good, or mean him harm,
Whensoever fate may bring you,
The vile snake will *always sting you.*

 2. View your child as weak-willed and your job as helping him strengthen his will to do what is right even when he doesn't feel like doing it.

Lesson 3

Discuss point three. Think of the restraint it takes to make oneself obey a command that doesn't seem particularly pleasant.

 3. Understand that obedience is a stepping-stone to self-control.

Activity: Have a little relay race in which your children have to carry a small object, such as a marshmallow or marble, on a spoon to the finish line and back without dropping the object. They must listen carefully for the word, "Go!" and control themselves not to start until they hear it. You can shout words that start with "go" such as "Gomer" or you could do rhyming words, such as "low," before getting to the word "go."

Lesson 4

Talk about point four and the quotation together. We are in a battle against our very selves when our wills are weak.

Habit points from *Laying Down the Rails*

4. Develop a sense of conquest over your weak will whenever you exercise self-control.

"Most powerful is he who has himself in his own power." — *Seneca*

Read James 3:1–12. Taming the tongue is no small feat; but if you can control your tongue, you'll be able to control yourself in other ways also.

Lesson 5

Discuss point seven and the poem below.

 7. Think hard on good thoughts and actions will follow.

5. Invite your child's cooperation in developing this habit within himself.

6. Watch for and applaud any efforts your child puts forth to control himself.

Words
from *Harper's Third Reader*, edited by James Baldwin

A little tender word,
    Wrapped in a little rhyme,
Sent out upon the passing air,
As seeds are scattered everywhere,
    In the sweet summertime.

A little idle word,
    Breathed in an idle hour,
Between two laughs that word was said,
Forgotten as soon as uttered,
    And yet the word had power.

Away they sped—the words;
    One, like a winged seed,
Lit on a soul that gave it room,
And straight began to bud and bloom
    In lovely word and deed.

The other careless word,
    Borne on an evil air,
Found a rich soil and ripened fast
Its rank and poisonous growth, and cast
    Fresh seeds to work elsewhere.

The speakers of the words
    Passed by and marked, one day,
The fragrant blossoms, dewy wet,
The baneful flowers, thickly set
    In clustering array.

And neither knew his word;
    One smiled, and one did sigh.
"How strange and sad," one said, "it is
That people do such things as this;
    I'm glad it was not I."

And "What a wondrous word
   To reach so far, so high!"
The other said. "What joy 'twould be
To send out words so helpfully;
   I wish that it were I."

Lesson 6

Passionate true words and actions can bring a person to repentance. Sometimes truth seems harsh, but speaking it does not mean you are out of control. Lies, curses, unnecessary harshness, name-calling, meanness—these have no place with Self-Control.

Read Mark 3:1–6 and Mark 11:15–18. In both of these instances, Jesus was angry; yet He did not sin. There is a righteous anger over sin that does not have to lead to out-of-control actions.

Lesson 7

Read and discuss the quotation.

> *"That which we persist in doing becomes easier, not that the task itself has become easier, but that our ability to perform it has improved." — Ralph Waldo Emerson*

Activity: Play a game in which each child is given a certain number of minutes to either stand very still in one spot, sit without moving, or walk a straight line back and forth (a line of tape on the floor makes a good tight rope). If they feel the need to laugh or turn their heads, they can work on changing their thoughts to keep themselves focused. You might tell jokes or make funny faces to make it more challenging for older children.

Lesson 8

Read and discuss the poem. Children will get plenty of practice with Self-Control if they have siblings or neighborhood children close to their age.

Against Quarrelling and Fighting
by Isaac Watts

Let dogs delight to bark and bite,
   For God has made them so;
Let bears and lions growl and fight,
   For 'tis their nature too.

But, children, you should never let
   Such angry passions rise;
Your little hands were never made
   To tear each other's eyes.

Let love through all your actions run,
   And all your words be mild;
Live like the blessed Virgin's Son,
   That sweet and lovely child.

8. Introduce and reinforce these principles little by little as opportunities arise.

His soul was gentle as a lamb;
    And as his stature grew,
He grew in favour both with man
    And God his Father too.

Now, Lord of all, he reigns above,
    And from his heavenly throne,
He sees what children dwell in love,
    And marks them for his own.

Lesson 9

Talk about the wisdom of bearing a single injury in silence instead of flying off in a rage. Read the Aesop fable for an illustration.

The Bear and the Bees
from *The Aesop for Children* by Milo Winter

A Bear roaming the woods in search of berries happened on a fallen tree in which a swarm of Bees had stored their honey. The Bear began to nose around the log very carefully to find out if the Bees were at home. Just then one of the swarm came home from the clover field with a load of sweets. Guessing what the Bear was after, the Bee flew at him, stung him sharply and then disappeared into the hollow log.

The Bear lost his temper in an instant, and sprang upon the log tooth and claw, to destroy the nest. But this only brought out the whole swarm. The poor Bear had to take to his heels, and he was able to save himself only by diving into a pool of water.

It is wiser to bear a single injury in silence than to provoke a thousand by flying into a rage.

Lesson 10

Talk about times when you are nervous and ways to overcome common reactions such as crying, stuttering, loud talking, and the like.

Read Esther 5:1–7 and chapter 7. Esther was nervous and afraid, yet she acted wisely and deliberately to gain the best attitude from the king. Contrast this self-control with Haman's craziness in chapter 7.

Lesson 11

Our outbursts of anger will bring heartache. Read and discuss the story below.

The King and His Hawk
from *Fifty Famous Stories Retold* by James Baldwin

Genghis Khan was a great king and warrior.

He led his army into China and Persia, and he conquered many lands. In every country, men told about his daring deeds; and they said that since Alexander the Great, there had been no king like him.

One morning when he was home from the wars, he rode out into the woods to have a day's sport. Many of his friends were with him. They rode out gayly, carrying their bows and arrows. Behind them came the servants with the hounds.

It was a merry hunting party. The woods rang with their shouts and laughter. They expected to carry much game home in the evening.

On the king's wrist sat his favorite hawk; for in those days hawks were trained to hunt. At a word from their masters they would fly high up into the air, and look around for prey. If they chanced to see a deer or a rabbit, they would swoop down upon it swift as any arrow.

All day long Genghis Khan and his huntsmen rode through the woods. But they did not find as much game as they expected.

Toward evening they started for home. The king had often ridden through the woods, and he knew all the paths. So while the rest of the party took the nearest way, he went by a longer road through a valley between two mountains.

The day had been warm, and the king was very thirsty. His pet hawk had left his wrist and flown away. It would be sure to find its way home.

The king rode slowly along. He had once seen a spring of clear water near this pathway. If he could only find it now! But the hot days of summer had dried up all the mountain brooks.

At last, to his joy, he saw some water trickling down over the edge of a rock. He knew that there was a spring farther up. In the wet season, a swift stream of water always poured down here; but now it came only one drop at a time.

The king leaped from his horse. He took a little silver cup from his hunting bag. He held it so as to catch the slowly falling drops.

It took a long time to fill the cup; and the king was so thirsty that he could hardly wait. At last it was nearly full. He put the cup to his lips, and was about to drink.

All at once there was a whirring sound in the air, and the cup was knocked from his hands. The water was all spilled upon the ground.

The king looked up to see who had done this thing. It was his pet hawk.

The hawk flew back and forth a few times, and then alighted among the rocks by the spring.

The king picked up the cup, and again held it to catch the trickling drops.

This time he did not wait so long. When the cup was half full, he lifted it toward his mouth. But before it had touched his lips, the hawk swooped down again, and knocked it from his hands.

And now the king began to grow angry. He tried again; and for the third time the hawk kept him from drinking.

The king was now very angry indeed.

"How do you dare to act so?" he cried. "If I had you in my hands, I would wring your neck!"

Then he filled the cup again. But before he tried to drink, he drew his sword.

"Now, Sir Hawk," he said, "this is the last time."

He had hardly spoken, before the hawk swooped down and knocked the cup from his hand. But the king was looking for this. With a quick sweep of the sword he struck the bird as it passed.

The next moment the poor hawk lay bleeding and dying at its master's feet.

"That is what you get for your pains," said Genghis Khan.

But when he looked for his cup he found that it had fallen between two rocks, where he could not reach it.

"At any rate, I will have a drink from that spring," he said to himself.

With that he began to climb the steep bank to the place from which the water trickled. It was hard work, and the higher he climbed, the thirstier he became.

At last he reached the place. There indeed was a pool of water; but what was that lying in the pool, and almost filling it? It was a huge, dead snake of the most poisonous kind.

The king stopped. He forgot his thirst. He thought only of the poor dead bird lying on the ground below him.

"The hawk saved my life!" he cried; "and how did I repay him? He was my best friend, and I have killed him."

He clambered down the bank. He took the bird up gently, and laid it in his hunting bag. Then he mounted his horse and rode swiftly home. He said to himself,—

"I have learned a sad lesson today; and that is, never to do anything in anger."

Lesson 12

Read and discuss the rhyme below.

> "If you your lips would keep from slips,
> Five things observe with care:
> To whom you speak; of whom you speak;
> And how, and when, and where." — William Norris

Have a Parent Share moment to share a story from your life or tell about a person who exemplifies Self-Control.

Lesson 13

Discuss how the following Scriptures relate to Self-Control.

Proverbs 14:29—Quick-tempered equals folly.
Proverbs 18:13—Listen before answering.
Galatians 5:22–25—Self-control is a fruit of the Spirit.
Ephesians 4:26, 27—In anger do not sin.
1 Thessalonians 5:6–8—Be alert and self-controlled.

Lesson 14

Read and discuss the quotation below, then finish up with any other discussion, ideas, or celebration your family enjoys. Keep up this habit while going forth to concentrate on a new one.

"We cannot always build the future for our youth, but we can build our youth for the future." — Franklin D. Roosevelt

Sweet, Even Temper

Making the best of things; looking on the bright side

Parent Prep

Read detailed thoughts about Sweet, Even Temper on pages 108–110 of *Laying Down the Rails* and skim the lessons below.

♦ Goals for this Habit (and steps to get there)

_____

_____

_____

♦ A Person or Story from My Life that Demonstrates this Habit

_____

_____

_____

♦ Additional Stories, Poems, Quotations, Bible Verses I Want to Use

_____

_____

_____

♦ Other Activities We Could Do to Practice this Habit

_____

_____

_____

♦ Celebration Ideas

_____

_____

_____

Lesson 1

Read the definition and discuss a Sweet, Even Temper. Share with the children any goals you've identified for this habit (for instance, "We will change our thoughts to pleasant, productive ones when complaining clouds our minds."). Also get their input on changes they think need to be made.

Read the Biblical principle found in Philippians 4:8–13 from your preferred version of the Bible. We are called to contentment and joy and keeping our thoughts on admirable things.

Notes

 1. Don't excuse a sullen temperament on the basis of heredity or age.

 2. Correct your child's tendency before it becomes a temper.

"Temper" refers to a person's state of mind.

Lesson 2

Discuss the quotation and point three together.

> *"Good thoughts bear good fruit, bad thoughts bear bad fruit—and man is his own gardener." — James Allen*

3. Redirect your sullen thoughts along good lines.

Activity: Let the children brainstorm ways to change their thinking when they start to get in a bad mood or are disappointed over deferred plans. Include actions like choosing an uplifting or fun song to listen to, reading a good book, working on a favorite hobby, doing something active like riding a bike, writing a letter, looking through old photos, etc. You might let them find their go-to song and listen to it, or have them make a personal master list.

Lesson 3

Read and discuss the fable below. There is much we can be thankful for when we're tempted to pity ourselves.

The Hares and the Frogs
from *The Aesop for Children* by Milo Winter

Hares, as you know, are very timid. The least shadow sends them scurrying in fright to a hiding place. Once, they decided to die rather than live in such misery. But while they were debating how best to meet death, they thought they heard a noise and in a flash were scampering off to the warren. On the way they passed a pond where a family of Frogs was sitting among the reeds on the bank. In an instant the startled Frogs were seeking safety in the mud.

"Look," cried a Hare, "things are not so bad after all, for here are creatures who are even afraid of us!"

However unfortunate we may think we are there is always someone worse off than ourselves.

Lesson 4

Read and discuss the quotation and poem.

> *"Cheerfulness and contentment are great beautifiers, and are famous preservers of good looks." — Charles Dickens*

The Prayer Perfect
by James Whitcomb Riley

Dear Lord! kind Lord!
  Gracious Lord! I pray
Thou wilt look on all I love,
  Tenderly today!
Weed their hearts of weariness;
  Scatter every care
Down a wake of angel-wings
  Winnowing the air.

 Habit points from *Laying Down the Rails*

Bring unto the sorrowing
    All release from pain;
Let the lips of laughter
    Overflow again;
And with all the needy
    O divide, I pray,
This vast treasure of content
    That is mine today!

Lesson 5

No one enjoys being around a complainer. Philippians 2:14 and 15 talks about doing everything without grumbling or complaining.

Read Numbers 21:4–9. Over and over again the Israelites complained against the very food and provisions God gave to them. After their repentance, God also provided a way for healing.

Lesson 6

Not only do grumpy people make life miserable for those around them, they also make themselves miserable and then blame others for their attitude. Read an example of this in "Miss Cloud and Miss Sunbeam."

Miss Cloud and Miss Sunbeam
adapted from *Harper's Third Reader*, edited by James Baldwin

My window overlooks a garden where two little girls play almost every day. I call one of them Miss Cloud, and the other Miss Sunbeam. The first makes a great friend of a pout, and twists her lips down. The other is always showing love with a smile, which gives to her sweet lips a pretty curve. Can you guess how they look?

The other day they went out into the woods and pastures for wild flowers; and when they came back they brought bunches of blue violets and daisies, and some green ferns which had already begun to wilt. They were very happy, and yet very tired, with muddy shoes and soiled, torn aprons.

Sunbeam gave some of her nicest flowers to her mother, and some to her sister. Miss Cloud said that she had worked too hard to give any of hers away—she wanted them all herself. But after eating supper, she forgot them, and the next morning they were found on the window sill, quite limp and dead. Sunbeam's had been put into water, and were now tossing their heads as gayly as if they were still in their shady beds in the woods.

"Let's play pony," said Miss Cloud.

"You may drive," said Miss Sunbeam.

"All right!" and away they went, as happy as two birds.

All at once one of the lines broke. Miss Cloud stamped her foot—

"We never play anything unless something happens!"

"I can fix it in a minute," said Sunbeam, smiling.

"The yard isn't big enough to play in, and we can't have any fun."

"Oh, I think we do very well," I heard Sunbeam answer.

"You are not a good pony, and I won't play any more," said Miss Cloud; and, with an ugly frown on her face, she ran into the house.

Notes

"The child is born, doubtless, with the tendencies which should shape his future; but every tendency has its branch roads, its good or evil outcome; and to put the child on the right track for the fulfillment of the possibilities inherent in him, *is the vocation of the parent" (Vol. 1, p. 109).*

Sunbeam played alone the rest of the day, and she was so happy, and all things out-of-doors were so bright, that she seemed like a real sunbeam playing with sunbeams.

Their mother wanted to surprise them one afternoon. When they came home from school they saw, under the apple tree in the yard, a table covered with a white cloth. On it were tiny cream-cakes, a small glass jar of honey, rice-cakes, and a tall dish of nuts and candy right in the center. How they laughed and cried with joy, and ran for their wax dolls and toy tea sets!

After it was all over, I heard Miss Cloud ask:

"Don't you hope that mother will give us another?"

"Oh, I don't think about another," said Sunbeam, "I think about this, it is so nice!" and her pretty face smiled all over with happiness.

These little girls are both my pets; but which do you think I like best? Which do you like best?

Lesson 7

God enjoys our laughter and knows that a good temper is good for us. Read and enjoy the poems below.

Dust of Snow
by Robert Frost

The way a crow
Shook down on me
The dust of snow
From a hemlock tree

Has given my heart
A change of mood
And saved some part
Of a day I had rued.

On Any Ordinary Man in a High State of Laughter and Delight
by James Whitcomb Riley

Let the old man laugh and be
Blest therefore eternally!

As it's give' me to perceive,
I most certin'y believe
When a man's jest glad plum' through,
God's pleased with him, same as you.

Lesson 8

Ecclesiastes 7:14 tells us to be happy when times are good and to consider when times are bad. God has made them both.

Activity: Be still. Take a few minutes to practice the art of being still and thinking on the good things in your life and the Author of those blessings. Provide a few Scriptures to be read silently or out loud, such as Psalm 34, 84, or 117.

Lesson 9

Proverbs 16:24 talks about pleasant words being sweet to the soul. A cheerful word or a cheerful look can change another's down-hearted perspective. Read and discuss the story below.

The Cricket
from *Harper's Third Reader*, edited by James Baldwin

Did you hear that?—"Cheer-up! Cheer-up!"—It was the cry of the cricket. Little Annie, who was sitting in an easy-chair before the fire, jumped down from her seat and began to look all around for the tiny creature.

"If I can catch you, Mr. Cricket," she said, "I will make you tell me what you mean by your song."

But it was not easy to catch him. He might be here or he might be there—nobody could be quite sure. "Cheer-up! Cheer-up!" he sang. "Cheer-up! Cheer-up!" happy and gay and safe in his hiding place near the hearth.

"Never mind, sir," said Annie, "I know what you look like. You are a little fellow about an inch long; and you wear a handsome coat of yellow and brown. You rub your wing-covers together and make that sound, 'Cheer-up! Cheer-up!' I know you do not make it with your mouth, Mr. Cricket!"

"Cheer-up! Cheer-up!" answered the cricket. But little Annie could not find his hiding place. "I read a pretty verse today about your cousin, the black cricket, who stays in the field. Shall I sing it to you?

"'The cricket lives in the cold, cold ground,
At the foot of an old oak tree,
And all through the frosty autumn night
A merry song sings he.
Then he whistles a clear and happy tune,
By the gentle light of the silver moon.
The winds may moan,
With a hollow tone,
Through the leaves of the rustling tree;
The clouds may fly across the blue sky,
The flowers may droop and the brook may sigh,
But not in the least cares he.
He whistles a clear and happy tune,
By the gentle light of the silver moon,
All through the frosty autumn night,
And not in the least cares he.'"

"Cheer-up! Cheer-up!" still sang the cricket, as though he were pleased with Annie's little song.

"Cheer-up! Cheer-up!" he seemed to say. "Even though it be cold and dark, and even though the wind does whistle, and the rain does fall—is it not better to sing than to cry?"

"I am sure that it is," answered Annie, as she climbed back into the easy-chair. Then she sang the rest of the song:

"'There's a tiny cricket within my heart,
And a pleasant song sings he;
He sings of the kindness and goodness of God,

Which He daily shows to me.
Let the cricket whistle loud and clear,
Never drive him away with a tear;
There's darkness enough on the earth, even now,
Without the gloom of a frowning brow.
Cheer up the heart that is clouded in night;
Tell it in words of love,
Of hope on earth, and a land all bright—
The land of life and love—
And never fret
When you cannot get
Just what you want while you travel here.'"

Lesson 10

When we accept God's plan, we are much more contented and joyful. Sometimes circumstances are a result of the ugliness sin brought into the world. But acceptance of circumstances can help us move past that ugliness and bring joy back into our lives.

Read 1 Samuel 23:7–18. Saul was pursuing David to kill him. Jonathan, Saul's son, met up with David and acknowledged that David would be the next king. He could have been resentful that David would take his place, but Jonathan's attitude was one of acceptance and great friendship instead.

Lesson 11

Read the Biblical principles found in 1 Thessalonians 5:16–18: Be joyful. Pray continually. Give thanks in all circumstances. Then read and discuss the poem below.

A Little Lesson
from *Harper's Third Reader*, edited by James Baldwin

Some little housekeepers, one day,
Were getting supper, just in play,
   And laughing very cheerily.
The grass a velvet carpet made
Beneath the green-leaved maple's shade;
   No room so pleasant nearly.

Then Carrie brought a napkin red;
"'Twill make a pretty cloth," she said.
   But when she came to try it,
Alas! 'twas not quite large enough
To hide the table, slightly rough—
   'Twas useless to deny it.

Then woeful looks and sad dismay
Began to chase the smiles away,
   So narrow did they find it;
Till out spoke sunny little Nell,

"We'll leave it so, 'tis just as well,
   And play we do not mind it."

The smiles came back once more;
Too soon the pleasant feast was o'er.
   For the shadows gathered quickly,
And a star shone silvery in the west,
Telling each merry little guest
   To seek the home-fold quickly.

The lesson is as plain as day;
A cloud may rise above your way,
   But sunshine is behind it.
When things go wrong and others frown,
Just put all vain complainings down,
   And play you do not mind it.

One little act of kindness done,
   One little kind word spoken,
Has power to make a thrill of joy
   E'en in a heart that's broken.

Lesson 12

Read and discuss the quotation below, then have a Parent Share moment to share a story from your life or tell about a person who exemplifies a Sweet, Even Temper.

"Happiness is a thing to be practiced, like the violin." — John Lubbock

Lesson 13

Discuss how these Scriptures relate to a Sweet, Even Temper.

Proverbs 14:30—Peace and tranquility gives life; envy rots the bones.
Proverbs 15:13—A happy heart makes the face cheerful.
Proverbs 15:16, 17—Love and the fear of the Lord bring contentment.
Proverbs 18:14—A man's spirit can sustain him in sickness.
1 Timothy 6:6–10—Be content with little.
Matthew 6:25–34—Do not worry.

Lesson 14

Read and discuss the story below, then finish up with any other discussion, ideas, or celebration your family enjoys. Keep up this habit while going forth to concentrate on a new one.

The Miller of the Dee
from *Fifty Famous Stories Retold* by James Baldwin

Once upon a time there lived on the banks of the River Dee a miller, who was the happiest man in England. He was always busy from morning till night, and he was always singing as merrily as any lark. He was so cheerful that he made everybody else cheerful; and people all over the land liked to talk about his pleasant ways. At last the king heard about him.

"I will go down and talk with this wonderful miller," he said. "Perhaps he can tell me how to be happy."

As soon as he stepped inside of the mill, he heard the miller singing:—

"I envy no-body—no, not I!—

For I am as happy as I can be;

And nobody envies me."

"You're wrong, my friend," said the king. "You're wrong as wrong can be. I envy you; and I would gladly change places with you, if I could only be as light-hearted as you are."

The miller smiled, and bowed to the king.

"I am sure I could not think of changing places with you, sir," he said.

"Now tell me," said the king, "what makes you so cheerful and glad here in your dusty mill, while I, who am king, am sad and in trouble every day."

The miller smiled again, and said, "I do not know why you are sad, but I can easily tell why I am glad. I earn my own bread; I love my wife and my children; I love my friends, and they love me; and I owe not a penny to any man. Why should I not be happy? For here is the River Dee, and every day it turns my mill; and the mill grinds the corn that feeds my wife, my babes, and me."

"Say no more," said the king. "Stay where you are, and be happy still. But I envy you. Your dusty cap is worth more than my golden crown. Your mill does more for you than my kingdom can do for me. If there were more such men as you, what a good place this world would be! Goodbye, my friend!"

The king turned about, and walked sadly away; and the miller went back to his work singing:—

"Oh, I'm as happy as happy can be,

For I live by the side of the River Dee!"

Truthfulness
Aligning words and actions in accordance with fact

Parent Prep

Read detailed thoughts about Truthfulness on pages 110–116 of *Laying Down the Rails* and skim the lessons below.

♦ Goals for this Habit (and steps to get there)

_____
_____
_____

♦ A Person or Story from My Life that Demonstrates this Habit

_____
_____
_____

♦ Additional Stories, Poems, Quotations, Bible Verses I Want to Use

_____
_____
_____

♦ Other Activities We Could Do to Practice this Habit

_____
_____
_____

♦ Celebration Ideas

_____
_____
_____

The habit of Truthfulness is one of the "Top Three" habits that Charlotte talked about most. The other two are Attention and Obedience.

Charlotte wrote directly to young people about Truthfulness in Volume 4, Book 1, pages 150–166.

Lesson 1

Read the definition and discuss Truthfulness. Share with the children any goals you've identified for this habit (for instance, "We will not exaggerate to get a laugh or to win someone over to our side."). Also get their input on changes they think need to be made.

Read the Biblical principle found in Ephesians 4:25 from your preferred version of the Bible. Being truthful is a matter of obedience to God's command, not just a matter of preference. (There are several more Scriptures on Truthfulness at the end of this habit section if you want to use them throughout your emphasis on Truthfulness.)

Lesson 2

Discuss point one together, talking about how telling the truth often takes courage. Read and discuss the story that follows.

 1. **State facts carefully and exactly, without leaving anything out or exaggerating.**

The Boy and the Robbers
from *Fifty Famous Stories* by James Baldwin

In Persia, when Cyrus the Great was king, boys were taught to tell the truth. This was one of their first lessons at home and at school.

"None but a coward will tell a falsehood," said the father of young Otanes.

"Truth is beautiful. Always love it," said his mother.

When Otanes was twelve years old, his parents wished to send him to a distant city to study in a famous school that was there. It would be a long journey and a dangerous one. So it was arranged that the boy should travel with a small company of merchants who were going to the same place. "Good-by, Otanes! Be always brave and truthful," said his father. "Farewell, my child! Love that which is beautiful. Despise that which is base," said his mother.

The little company began its long journey. Some of the men rode on camels, some on horses. They went but slowly, for the sun was hot and the way was rough.

Suddenly, towards evening, a band of robbers swooped down upon them. The merchants were not fighting men. They could do nothing but give up all their goods and money.

"Well, boy, what have you got?" asked one of the robbers, as he pulled Otanes from his horse.

"Forty pieces of gold" answered the lad.

The robber laughed. He had never heard of a boy with so much money as that.

"That is a good story" he said. "Where do you carry your gold?"

"It is in my hat, underneath the lining," answered Otanes.

"Oh, well! You can't make me believe that," said the robber; and he hurried away to rob one of the rich merchants.

Soon another came up and said, "My boy, do you happen to have any gold about you?"

"Yes! Forty pieces, in my hat," said Otanes.

"You are a brave lad to be joking with robbers," said the man; and he also hurried on to a more promising field.

At length the chief of the band called to Otanes and said, "Young fellow, have you anything worth taking?"

Otanes answered, "I have already told two of your men that I have forty pieces of gold in my hat. But they wouldn't believe me."

"Take off your hat," said the chief.

The boy obeyed. The chief tore out the lining and found the gold hidden beneath it.

"Why did you tell us where to find it?" he asked. "No one would have thought that a child like you had gold about him."

"If I had answered your questions differently, I should have told a lie," said Otanes; "and none but cowards tell lies."

The robber chief was struck by this answer. He thought of the number of times that he himself had been a coward. Then he said, "You are a brave boy, and you may keep your gold. Here it is. Mount your horse, and my own men will ride with you and see that you reach the end of your journey in safety."

Otanes, in time, became one of the famous men of his country. He was the advisor and friend of two of the kings who succeeded Cyrus.

Lesson 3

Talk over point three, thinking of examples of each of the three causes.

 3. Lying can come through being careless in gathering facts, careless in stating facts, or through a deliberate intention to deceive. Avoid all three causes, not just the third.

 2. Be scrupulous in requiring exact truth.

Read Luke 24:13–35. Two men were walking down the road when a strange man walked up and started talking with them. They accurately recounted the recent events of Jesus' death and disappearance without embellishing the truth. We can sometimes feel the need to exaggerate even an already amazing story for effect. Can you imagine exaggerating a story to a stranger who turns out to be Jesus? How embarrassing that would have been!

Lesson 4

Discuss point four and the quotation below.

> *"The most dangerous untruths are truths moderately distorted."* — *Georg Christoph Lichtenberg*

 4. Accuracy is required in both small and important matters.

Activity: Hold a "truth telling lesson" in which each child goes to a window or spot outside, and after attentively looking around, he comes back to tell you exactly what he saw, without omitting or exaggerating facts. You could ask for a sky picture or landscape or another object in nature.

Lesson 5

Consider point five together, then read and discuss the Aesop fable.

 5. Lying for the sake of humor is not excused.

The Shepherd Boy and the Wolf
from *The Aesop for Children* by Milo Winter

A Shepherd Boy tended his master's Sheep near a dark forest not far from the village. Soon he found life in the pasture very dull. All he could do to amuse himself was to talk to his dog or play on his shepherd's pipe.

One day as he sat watching the Sheep and the quiet forest, and thinking what he would do should he see a Wolf, he thought of a plan to amuse himself.

His Master had told him to call for help should a Wolf attack the flock, and the Villagers would drive it away. So now, though he had not seen anything that even looked like a Wolf, he ran toward the village shouting at the top of his voice, "Wolf! Wolf!"

As he expected, the Villagers who heard the cry dropped their work and ran in great excitement to the pasture. But when they got there they found the Boy doubled up with laughter at the trick he had played on them.

A few days later the Shepherd Boy again shouted, "Wolf! Wolf!" Again the Villagers ran to help him, only to be laughed at again. Then one evening as the sun was setting behind the forest and the shadows were creeping out over the pasture, a Wolf really did spring from the underbrush and fall upon the Sheep.

In terror the Boy ran toward the village shouting "Wolf! Wolf!" But though the Villagers heard the cry, they did not run to help him as they had before. "He cannot fool us again," they said.

The Wolf killed a great many of the Boy's sheep and then slipped away into the forest.

Liars are not believed even when they speak the truth.

Lesson 6

📖 *6. Treat deceit as a radical character defect that needs to be corrected rather than excused.*

📖 *7. Realize it is better to cultivate the habit of truth from the outset rather than have to deal with the bad consequences of lying.*

Discuss point eight. Remember to help each other speak accurately and truthfully throughout this habit training period. Don't be condemning of one another but encouraging. Read and discuss the poem below.

 8. Avoid qualifying your statements with "I think," or "I believe," or "perhaps." Instead, always speak accurately.

Truth Never Dies
Author Unknown

Truth never dies. The ages come and go.
    The mountains wear away, the stars retire.
Destruction lays earth's mighty cities low;
    And empires, states and dynasties expire;
But caught and handed onward by the wise,
    Truth never dies.

Though unreceived and scoffed at through the years,
    Though made the butt of ridicule and jest,
Though held aloft for mockery and jeers,
    Denied by those of transient power possessed,
Insulted by the insolence of lies,
    Truth never dies.

It answers not. It does not take offense,
    But with a mighty silence bides its time.
As some great cliff that braves the elements
    And lifts through all the storms its head sublime,
It ever stands, uplifted by the wise,
    And never dies.

As rests the Sphinx amid Egyptian sands;

> As looms on high the snowy peak and crest;
> As firm and patient as Gibraltar stands,
> So truth, unwearied, waits the era blest
> When men shall turn to it with great surprise.
> Truth never dies.

Lesson 7

Talk about point nine and the quotation together.

> *"When regard for truth has been broken down or even slightly weakened, all things will remain doubtful."* — *St. Augustine*

 9. Think carefully and make sure you are certain before you speak.

Read 1 Samuel chapter 3. Samuel was a boy and was given a message from the Lord to pass on to Eli. The message was bad news for Eli; but Samuel, despite his fear, told it fully.

Lesson 8

Discuss point ten. Common politeness requires that we assume a speaker means well.

 10. Do not constantly correct another person's comments in the name of truth.

Activity: Give each child a message to be told to another person in the household. The child must give the message exactly as he heard it. The person told should write down what was said to him and send the message back to you to be checked for accuracy.

Lesson 9

Talk about point eleven and the quotation below. Sometimes we exaggerate so people will think we're important, or to get someone else to go along with us, or to get a reaction that feeds our ego. Read and discuss "The Leap at Rhodes."

> *"The elegance of honesty needs no adornment."* — *Merry Browne*

 11. Do not exaggerate for purposes of manipulation.

The Leap at Rhodes
from *The Aesop for Children* by Milo Winter

A certain man who visited foreign lands could talk of little when he returned to his home except the wonderful adventures he had met with and the great deeds he had done abroad.

One of the feats he told about was a leap he had made in a city called Rhodes. That leap was so great, he said, that no other man could leap anywhere near the distance. A great many persons in Rhodes had seen him do it and would prove that what he told was true.

"No need of witnesses," said one of the hearers. "Suppose this city is Rhodes. Now show us how far you can jump."

Deeds count, not boasting words.

Lesson 10

Discuss point twelve, pointing out any examples of bias in a newspaper or commercial, social media or local gossip. If we can't be sure a report is absolutely true, we do not need to spread it.

 12. Do not spread rumors, but carefully sift what you read and hear.

Have a Parent Share moment to share a story from your life or tell about a person who exemplifies Truthfulness.

Lesson 11

Talk over point thirteen together. If you just love, love chocolate ice cream, then what words are left to express love for your grandmother? Also read and discuss the story that emphasizes that "Honesty is Best."

 13. Do not use excessive language for common situations.

Honesty is Best
from *Harper's Third Reader*, edited by James Baldwin

For four or five weeks Lewis had been bringing home very poor reports of his work at school. He had failed, day after day, in spelling. How he did wish that a word could always be spelled the way it sounded! Then, instead of writing the word *tough* with five letters, he might write it with three, thus: *tuf.* But his teacher only grew stricter and stricter every day, and his stock of demerits kept growing larger all the time.

"Too bad!" sighed his mother, as she looked over his reports.

"That will not do!" said his father. "No more pocket money, sir, until you can show something better than that!"

Lewis began to feel as if all the world had turned against him.

One day, when he had almost made up his mind that he could never spell, he did what I am ashamed to tell you about. He opened his book and peeped into it behind the desk lid. Were there two *l*'s? Did *i* come first, or *e*? He saw the letters clearly, and when the teacher called upon him, he spelled the word boldly.

"Right!" said the trusting teacher, with a smile which went straight to the boy's heart. Oh, how ashamed he was! and how very small he felt when he thought that he had kept his place without deserving to do so!

He did not run merrily home that night. He did not want to go out and play. He had been far happier with a black failure written against his name than he was now with the undeserved word of praise sounding in his ears; for then he had at least been honest, and had not failed in doing his duty.

That evening he told me the whole story, and ended by saying: "It has taught me a lesson, dear aunt. All fair, and no cheating, for me, after this. I would rather fail in my spelling, and be punished, than to feel as mean as I have felt today."

Lesson 12

Discuss point fourteen and the quotation below. It's not wise to share a strong opinion about a town after meeting two of its citizens or an opinion about an artist after seeing only one of his paintings.

 14. Do not generalize; it gives the false impression that you have more knowledge or experience than you actually have.

"A lie stands on one leg, the truth on two." — *Benjamin Franklin*

Activity: Play a draw-it-and-guess-it game. Write on cards the situations that are to be drawn, and let them be about a time when someone would be tempted to be untruthful: a stain on the carpet, a broken toy, exaggerating a story to get your friends to laugh, not delivering a message out of laziness, etc. Divide the group into two teams. One person from a team draws the situation and the other members of the team have to guess what is being drawn. When time is up, talk about the situation and how a person could be truthful, as well as possible consequences if he were not truthful.

Lesson 13

Talk about point fifteen. Read and discuss the George Washington quotation and the poem below.

"I hope I shall always possess firmness and virtue enough to maintain what I consider the most enviable of all titles, the character of an honest man." — *George Washington*

 15. Let simplicity, sincerity, and fidelity be emphasized in your life.

Lady Clare
by Alfred, Lord Tennyson

It was the time when lilies blow,
   And clouds are highest up in air.
Lord Ronald brought a lily-white doe
   To give his cousin, Lady Clare.

I trow they did not part in scorn:
   Lovers long betrothed were they;
They two will wed the morrow morn;
   God's blessing on the day!

"He does not love me for my birth
   Nor for my lands so broad and fair;
He loves me for my own true worth,
   And that is well," said Lady Clare.

In there came old Alice the nurse,
   Said, "Who was this that went from thee?"
"It was my cousin," said Lady Clare;
   "To-morrow he weds with me."

Notes

"Oh, God be thanked!" said Alice the nurse,
    "That all comes round so just and fair:
Lord Ronald is heir of all your lands,
    And you are not the Lady Clare."

"Are ye out of your mind, my nurse, my nurse,"
    Said Lady Clare, "that ye speak so wild?"
"As God's above," said Alice the nurse,
    "I speak the truth: you are my child.

The old earl's daughter died at my breast;
    I speak the truth, as I live by bread!
I buried her like my own sweet child,
    And put my child in her stead."

"Falsely, falsely have ye done,
    O mother," she said, "if this be true,
To keep the best man under the sun
    So many years from his due."

"Nay now, my child," said Alice the nurse,
    "But keep the secret for your life,
And all you have will be Lord Ronald's,
    When you are man and wife."

"If I'm a beggar born," she said
    "I will speak out, for I dare not lie,
Pull off, pull off the brooch of gold,
    And fling the diamond necklace by."

"Nay now, my child," said Alice the nurse,
    "But keep the secret all you can."
She said, "Not so; but I will know
    If there be any faith in man."

"Nay now, what faith?" said Alice the nurse,
    "The man will cleave unto his right."
"And he shall have it," the lady replied,
    "Though I should die to-night."

"Yet give one kiss to your mother, dear!
    Alas, my child! I sinned for thee."
"O mother, mother, mother," she said,
    "So strange it seems to me!

Yet here's a kiss for my mother dear,
    My mother dear, if this be so,
And lay your hand upon my head,
    And bless me, mother, ere I go."

She clad herself in a russen gown,
  She was no longer Lady Clare:
She went by dale, and she went by down,
  With a single rose in her hair.

The lily-white doe Lord Ronald had brought
  Leapt up from where she lay,
Dropped her head in the maiden's hand,
  And followed her all the way.

Down stepped Lord Ronald from his tower:
  "O Lady Clare, you shame your worth!
Why come you dressed like a village maid,
  That are the flower of the earth?"

"If I come dressed like a village maid,
  I am but as my fortunes are:
I am a begger born," she said,
  "And not the Lady Clare."

"Play me no tricks," said Lord Ronald,
  "For I am yours in word and in deed;
Play me no tricks," said Lord Ronald,
  "Your riddle is hard to read."

Oh, and proudly stood she up!
  Her heart within her did not fail:
She looked into Lord Ronald's eyes,
  And told him all her nurse's tale.

He laughed a laugh of merry scorn:
  He turned and kissed her where she stood;
"If you are not the heiress born,
  And I," said he, "the next in blood—

If you are not the heiress born,
  And I," said he, "the lawful heir,
We two will wed to-morrow morn,
  And you shall still be Lady Clare."

Lesson 14

Finish up with any other discussion, ideas, or celebration your family enjoys. Keep up this habit while going forth to concentrate on a new one.

Use some of the following Scriptures to talk about the importance of Truthfulness.

    Deuteronomy 25:13–16—Have honest and accurate weights and measures.
    Proverbs 24:26—An honest answer is pleasing.
    Proverbs 25:13—Truthfulness is refreshing.

Matthew 5:33–37—There should be no need to take extra measures to assure listeners of the honesty of your words.

Luke 19:1–10—Zacchaeus paid back four-fold the amount he had cheated anyone.

Acts 5:1–11—God dealt swiftly with a married couple who conspired to lie.

Usefulness
Offering valuable or productive service

Parent Prep

Read detailed thoughts about Usefulness on pages 117–119 of *Laying Down the Rails* and skim the lessons below.

♦ Goals for this Habit (and steps to get there)

_____

_____

_____

♦ A Person or Story from My Life that Demonstrates this Habit

_____

_____

_____

_____

♦ Additional Stories, Poems, Quotations, Bible Verses I Want to Use

_____

_____

_____

_____

♦ Other Activities We Could Do to Practice this Habit

_____

_____

_____

_____

♦ Celebration Ideas

_____

_____

_____

Lesson 1

Read the definition and discuss Usefulness. Share with the children any goals you've identified for this habit (for instance, "We will look for opportunities to be useful whether at home or away."). Also get their input on changes they think need to be made.

Read the Biblical principle found in Ephesians 2:10 from your preferred version of the Bible. God created us with talents, and He also prepared works for which we could use those talents.

1. Help your child carry out his good intentions to actions.

Lesson 2

Discuss point two together, then read and discuss the poem that follows.

 2. **Older children can make themselves useful in caring for younger siblings, running errands, and helping with school work.**

Taking Care of Baby
from *The Infant's Delight*

Little, helpless baby dear,
   While within your cot you lie,
Sister May is sitting near—
   She will sing your lullaby.

When at last you fall asleep,
   Not the slightest noise she'll make;
Quiet as a mouse she'll keep,
   Lest she should her darling wake.

May will watch you well, for though
   She can play and prattle too,
'Tis not very long ago
   Since she was a babe like you.

Then mamma o'er little May
   Day and night her watch would keep;
May her care can now repay,
   Watching baby whilst asleep.

Feed minds. Inspire hearts. Encourage action.

Lesson 3

Talk about point three and the quotation below.

 3. **Love is shown by acts of service.**

"Enough, if something from our hands have power,
To live and act and serve the future hour." — Wordsworth

Read Acts 9:36–43. A disciple had spent her time doing good and helping the poor, so she was badly missed when she died.

When utilizing Bible passages, you could also read the story for yourself and do a delightful retelling. For younger children, you could use a Bible storybook such as Egermeier's Bible Story Book or Catherine Vos' The Child's Story Bible for some of the suggested Bible stories.

Lesson 4

Talk over point four. Read and discuss "Which Loved Best?"

 4. **As you grow older, you may be less inclined to demonstrate love for your parents physically, in hugs and kisses; but acts of service can still exhibit love.**

📖 Habit points from *Laying Down the Rails*

Which Loved Best?
by Joy Allison

"I love you mother," said little John;
Then, forgetting work his cap went on,
And he was off to the garden swing,
Leaving his mother the wood to bring.

"I love you, mother," said rosy Nell;
"I love you better than tongue can tell;"
Then she teased and pouted full half the day,
Till her mother rejoiced when she went to play.

"I love you, mother," said little Fran;
"today I'll help you all I can;
How glad I am that school doesn't keep!"
So she rocked the baby till it fell asleep.

Then stepping softly, she took the broom,
And swept the floor, and dusted the room;
Busy and happy all day was she,
Helpful and cheerful as child could be.

"I love you, mother," again they said—
Three little children going to bed;
How do you think that mother guessed
Which of them really loved her best?

Lesson 5

Discuss point five, then read and discuss the story that follows.

 5. Working hard to be useful now will prepare you to fulfill your calling in the future.

Our First Great Painter
from *Fifty Famous People* by James Baldwin

A long time ago there lived, in Pennsylvania, a little boy whose name was Benjamin West.

This boy loved pictures. Indeed, there were few things that he loved more. But he had never seen any pictures except a few small ones in a book.

His father and mother were Quakers, and they did not think it was right to spend money for such things. They thought that pictures might take one's mind away from things that were better or more useful.

One day Benjamin's mother had to go to a neighbor's on some errand. So she told Benjamin to stay in the house and take care of his baby sister till she came back.

He was glad to do this; for he loved the baby.

"Yes, mother," he said, "I will watch her every minute. I won't let anything hurt her."

The baby was asleep in her cradle, and he must not make a noise and waken her.

For some time he sat very still. He heard the clock ticking. He heard the birds singing. He began to feel a little lonesome.

A fly lighted on the baby's cheek, and he brushed it away. Then he thought what a pretty picture might be made of his sister's sweet face and little hands.

He had no paper, but he knew where there was a smooth board. He had no pencil, but there was a piece of black charcoal on the hearth. How pretty the baby was! He began to draw. The baby smiled but did not wake up.

As often as he touched the charcoal to the smooth board, the picture grew. Here was her round head, covered with pretty curls. Here was her mouth. Here were her eyes, and here her dainty ears. Here was her fat little neck. Here were her wonderful hands.

So busy was he with the drawing that he did not think of anything else. He heard neither the clock nor the birds. He did not even hear his mother's footsteps as she came into the room. He did not hear her soft breathing as she stood over him and watched him finish the wonderful drawing.

"O Benjamin! what has thee been doing?" she cried.

The lad sprang up alarmed.

"It's only a picture of the baby, mother," he said.

"A picture of the baby! Oh, wonderful! It looks just like her!"

The good woman was so overjoyed that she caught him in her arms and kissed him. Then suddenly she began to wonder whether this was right.

"Benjamin, how did thee learn to draw such a picture?" she asked.

"I didn't learn," he answered. "I just did it. I couldn't help but do it."

When Benjamin's father came home, his mother showed him the picture.

"It looks just like her, doesn't it?" she said. "But I am afraid. I don't know what to think. Does thee suppose that it is very wrong for Benjamin to do such a thing?"

The father did not answer. He turned the picture this way and that, and looked at it from every side. He compared it with the baby's pretty face. Then he handed it back to his wife and said:—

"Put it away. It may be that the hand of the Lord is in this."

Several weeks afterward, there came a visitor to the home of the Wests. It was a good old Friend, whom everybody loved—a white-haired, pleasant-faced minister, whose words were always wise.

Benjamin's parents showed him the picture. They told him how the lad was always trying to draw something. And they asked what they should do about it.

The good minister looked at the picture for a long time. Then he called little Benjamin to him. He put his hands on the lad's head and said:—

"This child has a wonderful gift. We cannot understand it nor the reason of it. Let us trust that great good may come from it, and that Benjamin West may grow up to be an honor to our country and the world."

And the words of the old minister came true. The pictures of Benjamin West made him famous. He was the first great American painter.

Lesson 6

We must be content and useful in little areas of service and we will be ready for big areas of service if God sees the need to call us there.

Read Genesis 39:1–6, 39:20–23, and 41:39–43. Joseph, as a slave and prisoner, faithfully and diligently served. Soon enough, he was out of prison and the pharaoh himself put Joseph in charge of the kingdom as second-in-command of Egypt.

Lesson 7

Our deeds may not always be successful, but do not let that stop you from trying. Read and discuss the story of "Thomas Hovenden—Artist."

Thomas Hovenden—Artist
from *An American Book of Golden Deeds* by James Baldwin

Hovenden was an American artist, although his birthplace was in Ireland. He had studied under the best masters, both in this country and in Paris. After years of effort and of faithful endeavor, fame and fortune seemed to be within his grasp; a life's ambition was almost realized.

One afternoon in August, 1895, he left his country home near Norristown, intending to ride by trolley to the railroad station where he would take the evening train for Philadelphia. At the outskirts of the town the passengers were required to alight from the first trolley car, cross the railroad tracks, and take another car on the opposite side.

Thomas Hovenden was one of the last to step out of the trolley car, and as he did so he heard the roar of a fast-freight train coming with great speed down the tracks in front of him. At the same time, to his great horror, he saw a little girl, who had been on the trolley, run forward to cross the railroad. The child had not noticed the approaching train, and was intent only upon reaching the second trolley car on the farther side of the tracks.

The engineer whistled. The child looked up and saw the great engine bearing down upon her. She was paralyzed with fear. She stood motionless between the tracks.

Then it was that Thomas Hovenden, fifty-five years of age, did the heroic deed of his life. Quicker than thought, he leaped forward and seized the child. Another second for another leap, and both of them would have been in safety. But, alas, the monster engine was too quick for him. It struck him as he was almost across. Artist and child were hurled far to the side of the road. They lay there in the dust, side by side, and quite motionless.

Gentle hands hastened to lift them up. But Thomas Hovenden, artist, hero, was dead. The child for whom he had given his life was unconscious. They lifted her from the ground; they carried her lovingly to a neighboring house; but before the sun went down that day, she too, had ceased to breathe. Shall we believe that Thomas Hovenden's golden deed was a failure? Far nobler is it to die in the attempt to save another's life than to live as a selfish coward afraid to perform one's duty to humanity. This last act of Thomas Hovenden proved him to be a hero of the noblest type; it crowned with the highest honor his already successful life.

Lesson 8

Ephesians 4:28 talks about doing something useful with our hands so that we can share with those in need.

Activity: Let your children think of a specific way they can be useful today. It could be playing with the baby, making lunch, setting the table, making someone's bed, picking up toys (even if they didn't get them out), weeding the garden, etc. Help them carry through with their plans. When the day closes, discuss what they did, how helpful it was, and the appreciation felt by the person helped.

Lesson 9

God made each person special. Each child (and adult) possesses some ability, personality, or trait that is unique to him or her. It is better to search for that possession in oneself and use it rather than try to poorly imitate what someone else does well. Read and discuss the poem below.

Envy
by Charles Lamb

This rose-tree is not made to bear
The violet blue, nor lily fair,
   Nor the sweet mignonette:
And if this tree were discontent,
Or wished to change its natural bent,
   It all in vain would fret.

And should it fret, you would suppose
It ne'er had seen its own red rose,
   Nor after gentle shower
Had ever smelled its rose's scent,
Or it could ne'er be discontent
   With its own pretty flower.

Like such a blind and senseless tree
As I've imagined this to be,
   All envious persons are:
With care and culture all may find
Some pretty flower in their own mind,
   Some talent that is rare.

Lesson 10

Continue the discussion from the previous lesson, identifying unique talents that each person in the family possesses.

Read Romans 12:3–8, 1 Peter 4:10 and 11, and 1 Corinthians 12:12–30. All the members of the Body of Christ have places of service within the church. Some jobs may seem more important than others. Indeed some jobs are higher profile, but every area of service is important. Eagerly desire to serve God with the gifts He blesses you with.

Lesson 11

Proverbs 22:29 tells us that a man skilled in his work will serve before high ranking men. We are given talents, but we must practice them in order for them to be sharpened and honed.

Activity: Discuss the different ways that each stage of life can be a useful one. Your children can choose one of the stages and draw a picture representing a person being useful or they can act out how that person is useful. The different stages include baby, toddler, young child, older child, young adult, middle-aged adult, retired adult, and very elderly.

Lesson 12

God established the family as the foundational institution. Our family members come first if they are in need of our services. Church, neighborhood, town, country, the world—these are other areas of service. Read and discuss "The King and the Page."

The King and the Page
from *Fifty Famous People* by James Baldwin

Many years ago there was a king of Prussia, whose name was Frederick; and because he was very wise and very brave, people called him Frederick the Great. Like other kings, he lived in a beautiful palace and had many officers and servants to wait upon him.

Among the servants there was a little page whose name was Carl. It was Carl's duty to sit outside of the king's bedroom and be ready to serve him at any time.

One night the king sat up very late, writing letters and sending messages; and the little page was kept busy running on errands until past midnight.

The next morning the king wished to send him on another errand. He rang the little bell which was used to call the page, but no page answered.

"I wonder what can have happened to the boy," he said; and he opened the door and looked out. There, sitting in his chair, was Carl, fast asleep. The poor child was so tired after his night's work that he could not keep awake.

The king was about to waken him roughly, when he saw a piece of paper on the floor beside him. He picked it up and read it.

It was a letter from the page's mother:—

"Dearest Carl; You are a good boy to send me all your wages, for now I can pay the rent and buy some warm clothing for your little sister. I thank you for it, and pray that God will bless you. Be faithful to the king and do your duty."

The king went back to the room on tiptoe. He took ten gold pieces from his table and wrapped them in the little letter. Then he went out again, very quietly, and slipped them all into the boy's pocket.

After a while he rang the bell again, very loudly.

Carl awoke with a start, and came quickly to answer the call.

"I think you have been asleep," said the king.

The boy stammered and did not know what to say. He was frightened and ready to cry.

He put his hand in his pocket, and was surprised to find the gold pieces wrapped in his mother's letter. Then his eyes overflowed with tears, and he fell on his knees before the king.

"What is the matter?" asked Frederick.

"Oh, your Majesty!" cried Carl. "Have mercy on me. It is true that I have been asleep, but I know nothing about this money. Some one is trying to ruin me."

"Have courage, my boy," said the king. "I know how you must have been overwearied with long hours of watching. And people say that fortune comes to us in our sleep. You may send the gold pieces to your mother with my compliments; and tell her that the king will take care of both her and you."

Lesson 13

Have a Parent Share moment to share a story from your life or tell about a person who exemplifies Usefulness. Read and discuss the rhyme below.

"Do all the good you can
By all the means you can
In all the ways you can
To all the people you can
As long as ever you can." — John Wesley

Lesson 14

Finish up with any other discussion, ideas, or celebration your family enjoys. Keep up this habit while going forth to concentrate on a new one.

Physical Habits

Alertness to Seize Opportunities
Being aware of ways to serve in your surroundings and taking the initiative to do them

Parent Prep

Read detailed thoughts about Alertness to Seize Opportunities on pages 122 and 123 of *Laying Down the Rails* and skim the lessons below.

♦ Goals for this Habit (and steps to get there)

_____

_____

_____

♦ A Person or Story from My Life that Demonstrates this Habit

_____

_____

_____

♦ Additional Stories, Poems, Quotations, Bible Verses I Want to Use

_____

_____

_____

♦ Other Activities We Could Do to Practice this Habit

_____

_____

_____

_____

♦ Celebration Ideas

_____

_____

_____

Choose the best way for your family to work through the habits in this book: 1) Pick and choose what seems most needed; 2) First do the top three recommended by Charlotte Mason—obedience, attention, and truthfulness; 3) Go through them in the order presented here in the book; 4) Rotate through the five categories—decency and propriety, mental, moral, physical, and religious—selecting one from each category in its turn.

Lesson 1

Read the definition and discuss Alertness to Seize Opportunities. Share with the children any goals you've identified for this habit (for instance, "We will open the door for any person who has their hands full, whether at home or out in public."). Also get their input on changes they think need to be made.

Read the Biblical principle found in James 2:15 and 16 from your preferred version of the Bible. Good intentions and dreams about great feats of accomplishment do not make a life of usefulness. You must act on the needs you see around you.

Lesson 2

Discuss point one together. Mention roadblocks that keep us from helping (for instance, laziness, fear, uncertainty) and discuss ways to overcome them. Then read and discuss the poem below.

 1. **Watch for and do not miss opportunities to help, such as delivering a message or opening a door.**

Wishing
by Ella Wheeler Wilcox

Do you wish the world were better?
　Let me tell you what to do.
Set a watch upon your actions,
　Keep them always straight and true.
Rid your mind of selfish motives,
　Let your thoughts be clean and high.
You can make a little Eden
　Of the sphere you occupy.

Do you wish the world were wiser?
　Well, suppose you make a start,
By accumulating wisdom
　In the scrapbook of your heart;
Do not waste one page on folly;
　Live to learn, and learn to live.
If you want to give men knowledge
　You must get, ere you give.

Do you wish the world were happy?
　Then remember day by day
Just to scatter seeds of kindness
　As you pass along the way,
For the pleasures of the many
　May be ofttimes traced to one,
As the hand that plants an acorn
　Shelters armies from the sun.

Lesson 3

Talk over point two, then read and discuss "Columbus and the Egg."

🖼 2. Watch as diligently for opportunities to learn.

Columbus and the Egg
from *Thirty More Famous Stories Retold* by James Baldwin

Christopher Columbus discovered America on the 12th of October, 1492. He had spent eighteen years in planning for that wonderful first voyage which he made across the Atlantic Ocean. The thoughts and hopes of the best part of his life had been given to it. He had talked and argued with sailors and scholars and princes and kings, saying, "I know that, by sailing west across the great ocean, one may at last reach lands that have never been visited by Europeans." But he had been laughed at as a foolish dreamer, and few people had any faith in his projects.

At last, however, the king and queen of Spain gave him ships with which to make the trial voyage. He crossed the ocean and discovered strange lands, inhabited by a people unlike any that had been known before. He believed that these lands were a part of India.

When he returned home with the news of his discovery there was great rejoicing, and he was hailed as the hero who had given a new world to Spain. Crowds of people lined the streets through which he passed, and all were anxious to do him honor. The king and queen welcomed him to their palace and listened with pleasure to the story of his voyage. Never had so great respect been shown to any common man.

But there were some who were jealous of the discoverer, and as ready to find fault as others were to praise. "Who is this Columbus?" they asked, "and what has he done? Is he not a pauper pilot from Italy? And could not any other seaman sail across the ocean just as he has done?"

One day Columbus was at a dinner which a Spanish gentleman had given in his honor, and several of these persons were present. They were proud, conceited fellows, and they very soon began to try to make Columbus uncomfortable.

"You have discovered strange lands beyond the sea," they said. "But what of that? We do not see why there should be so much said about it. Anybody can sail across the ocean; and anybody can coast along the islands on the other side, just as you have done. It is the simplest thing in the world."

Columbus made no answer; but after a while he took an egg from a dish and said to the company, "Who among you, gentlemen, can make this egg stand on end?"

One by one those at the table tried the experiment. When the egg had gone entirely around and none had succeeded, all said that it could not be done.

Then Columbus took the egg and struck its small end gently upon the table so as to break the shell a little. After that there was no trouble in making it stand upright.

"Gentlemen," said he, "what is easier than to do this which you said was impossible? It is the simplest thing in the world. Anybody can do it—after he has been shown how."

🖼 *3. Equip your child for success by cultivating this habit early in life.*

Lesson 4

Alertness implies quick thinking. If you over-think an opportunity, it will soon pass.

Read Exodus 2:1–10. Miriam quickly used the good fortune of the pharaoh's daughter's compassion to gain permission for her own mother to raise Moses.

Lesson 5

Read and discuss the quotation below.

"Human felicity is produced not so much by great pieces of good fortune that seldom happen, as by little advantages that occur every day." — *Benjamin Franklin*

Activity: Prepare a snack or tea time, or use this idea with clean-up, yard work, meal prep, etc. Instruct your children beforehand to look for ways they can help, but do not give specific directions about what needs to be done. Let them know that you want them to figure out what they can do and offer to do that action. You could also go grocery shopping and pause regularly in the various stages to tell the children to look around and suggest what needs to be done next, as well as ways they might be able to help accomplish those needs without waiting to be told.

Lesson 6

Don't pass by small opportunities because you're waiting for your big break. Read and discuss the quotation and the poem that follows.

"This could but have happened once,
And we missed it, lost it forever." — Robert Browning

Little Things
by Julia Fletcher Carney

Little drops of water,
    Little grains of sand,
Make the mighty ocean
    And the pleasant land.

So the little moments,
    Humble though they be,
Make the mighty ages
    Of eternity.

So the little errors
    Lead the soul away
From the paths of virtue
    Far in sin to stray.

Little deeds of kindness,
    Little words of love,
Help to make earth happy
    Like the Heaven above.

Lesson 7

Knowing right from wrong ahead of time helps with immediate action because you will not have to waste time figuring it out. Read and discuss "The Last Fight in the Coliseum."

The Last Fight in the Coliseum
adapted from *A Book of Golden Deeds* by Charlotte M. Yonge

The enemies of Rome were coming nearer and nearer, and Alaric, the great chief of the Goths, led his forces into Italy, and threatened the city itself. Honorius, the Emperor, was a cowardly, almost idiotical, boy; but his brave general, Stilicho, assembled his forces, met the Goths at Pollentia (about twenty-five miles from where Turin now stands), and gave them a complete defeat on the Easter Day of the year 403. He pursued them into the mountains, and for that time saved Rome. In the joy of the victory the Roman senate invited the conqueror and his ward Honorius to enter the city in triumph, at the opening of the new year, with the white steeds, purple robes, and vermilion cheeks with which, of old, victorious generals were welcomed at Rome. The churches were visited instead of the Temple of Jupiter, and there was no murder of the captives; but Roman bloodthirstiness was not yet allayed, and, after all the procession had been completed, the Coliseum shows commenced, innocently at first, with races on foot, on horseback, and in chariots; then followed a grand hunting of beasts turned loose in the arena; and next a sword dance. But after the sword dance came the arraying of swordsmen, with no blunted weapons, but with sharp spears and swords—a gladiator combat in full earnest. The people, enchanted, applauded with shouts of ecstasy this gratification of their savage tastes. Suddenly, however, there was an interruption. A rude, roughly robed man, bareheaded and barefooted, had sprung into the arena, and, signing back the gladiators, began to call aloud upon the people to cease from the shedding of innocent blood, and not to requite God's mercy in turning away the sword of the enemy by encouraging murder. Shouts, howls, cries broke in upon his words; this was no place for preachings—the old customs of Rome should be observed 'Back, old man!' 'On, gladiators!' The gladiators thrust aside the meddler, and rushed to the attack. He still stood between, holding them apart, striving in vain to be heard. 'Sedition! Sedition!' 'Down with him!' was the cry; and the man in authority, Alypius, the prefect, himself added his voice. The gladiators, enraged at interference with their vocation, cut him down. Stones, or whatever came to hand, rained down upon him from the furious people, and he perished in the midst of the arena! He lay dead, and then came the feeling of what had been done.

His dress showed that he was one of the hermits who vowed themselves to a holy life of prayer and self-denial, and who were greatly reverenced, even by the most thoughtless. The few who had previously seen him, told that he had come from the wilds of Asia on pilgrimage, to visit the shrines and keep his Christmas at Rome—they knew he was a holy man—no more, and it is not even certain whether his name was Alymachus or Telemachus. His spirit had been stirred by the sight of thousands flocking to see men slaughter one another, and in his simple-hearted zeal he had resolved to stop the cruelty or die. He had died, but not in vain. His work was done. The shock of such a death before their eyes turned the hearts of the people; they saw the wickedness and cruelty to which they had blindly surrendered themselves; and from the day when the hermit died in the Coliseum there was never another fight of the Gladiators. Not merely at Rome, but in every province of the Empire, the custom was utterly abolished; and one habitual crime at least was wiped from the earth by the self-devotion of one humble, obscure, almost nameless man.

Lesson 8

Talk about the difference between tattling and informing adults about serious harm that could befall someone.

Read Acts 23:12–24. A young man heard of a plot to kill Paul and told it to the proper people, saving Paul's life from treachery.

Lesson 9

Read and discuss the quotation below.

> *"Opportunity is missed by most people because it is dressed in overalls and looks like work." — Thomas Edison*

Activity: Play a game in which you or a child tries to do something precarious and the other children will need to step in to help. Here are some possibilities. Over a carpeted area, carry a pile of dishes that are stacked so as to fall at any moment (plates stacked on top of mugs, etc). Place a plate on your head and several in your hands and forearms and try to walk through a closed door. Race from one end of the house to the other trying to pick up toys and put them into an already overflowing basket. Carry a huge stack of books while walking through a room full of furniture or objects on the floor. Each child could think of his or her own precarious situation and give it a try while the rest of the family steps in to help.

Lesson 10

Read and discuss Mark 10:42–45. Jesus explained that a person of true greatness is a servant of all. Read and discuss the poem below.

Song of Life
by Charles Mackay

A traveler on a dusty road
    Strewed acorns on the lea;
And one took root and sprouted up,
    And grew into a tree.
Love sought its shade at evening time,
    To breathe its early vows;
And Age was pleased, in heights of noon,
    To bask beneath its boughs.
The dormouse loved its dangling twigs,
    The birds sweet music bore,
It stood a glory in its place,
    A blessing evermore.

A little spring had lost its way
    Amid the grass and fern;
A passing stranger scooped a well
    Where weary men might turn.
He walled it in, and hung with care
    A ladle on the brink;

He thought not of the deed he did,
  But judged that Toil might drink.
He passed again; and lo! the well,
  By summer never dried,
Had cooled ten thousand parched tongues,
  And saved a life beside.

A nameless man, amid the crowd
  That thronged the daily mart,
Let fall a word of hope and love,
  Unstudied from the heart.
A whisper of the tumult thrown,
  A transitory breath,
It raised a brother from the dust,
  It saved a soul from death.
O germ! O fount! O word of love!
  O thought at random cast!
Ye were but little at the first,
  But mighty at the last.

Lesson 11

Use wisdom to discern true need versus coercion or manipulation. It's easy for compassion to be manipulated. Of course, it might be best to err on the side of compassion and let God sort it out.

Read Luke 10:25–37. Jesus told a story about a lower-class man who physically and financially helped a beaten man whom others had passed by. This ill-treated man probably would not have lived without someone coming to his aid.

Lesson 12

Have a Parent Share moment to share a story from your life or tell about a person who exemplifies Alertness to Seize Opportunities. Read and discuss the quotation below.

> *"I was seldom able to see an opportunity until it had ceased to be one."* — *Mark Twain*

Finish up with any other discussion, ideas, or celebration your family enjoys. Keep up this habit while going forth to concentrate on a new one.

Fortitude

Bearing hardship or discomfort with courage

Parent Prep

Read detailed thoughts about Fortitude on pages 123–127 of *Laying Down the Rails* and skim the lessons below.

- ◆ Goals for this Habit (and steps to get there)

_____

_____

_____

- ◆ A Person or Story from My Life that Demonstrates this Habit

_____

_____

_____

- ◆ Additional Stories, Poems, Quotations, Bible Verses I Want to Use

_____

_____

_____

_____

Charlotte wrote directly to young people about Fortitude in Volume 4, Book 2, pages 41–48.

- ◆ Other Activities We Could Do to Practice this Habit

_____

_____

_____

_____

- ◆ Celebration Ideas

_____

_____

_____

_____

Lesson 1

Read the definition and discuss Fortitude. Share with the children any goals you've identified for this habit (for instance, "We will provide distractions and expect fortitude while hair is being combed and fixed."). Also get their input on changes they think need to be made.

Read the Biblical principle found in Hebrews 12:3–13 from your preferred version of the Bible. Painful circumstances happen in life. Painful cuts and scrapes and bone breaks happen too. Bearing up under such discomforts strengthens our resolve, our inner core.

God even tells us that he sends hardships to train us or discipline us.

Lesson 2

Discuss point one, coming up with examples of physical fortitude and mental fortitude.

 1. Fortitude in dealing with physical sensations can help develop mental fortitude.

Activity: Display several sizes of weights, such as hand weights, or put out different-sized cans of food. Let the children carefully try to lift each one. Talk about how you must start with small weights as you exercise before you move up to heavier ones. Likewise, as you build Fortitude with little pains—such as getting your tangled hair brushed, skinning your knee, being thirsty at the playground, or finishing a tiring hike—you will be ready for heavier discomforts that come your way.

Lesson 3

Talk together about point two. Read and discuss the quotation, making sure the children know who Helen Keller was.

> *"We could never learn to be brave and patient, if there were only joy in the world."*
> — *Helen Keller*

 2. Bear discomfort courageously.

Read Acts 16:16–40. Despite being severely flogged and imprisoned, Paul and Silas prayed and sang hymns to God while the other prisoners listened. They knew their hardship was brought on by preaching the gospel, and they were glad to suffer for Jesus' name.

Lesson 4

Talk about point three together. Read and discuss "Bruce and the Spider."

 3. Concentrate on other things rather than the discomfort.

Bruce and the Spider
from *Fifty Famous Stories* by James Baldwin

There was once a king of Scotland whose name was Robert Bruce. He had need to be both brave and wise, for the times in which he lived were wild and rude. The King of England was at war with him, and had led a great army into Scotland to drive him out of the land.

Battle after battle had been fought. Six times had Bruce led his brave little army against his foes; and six times had his men been beaten, and driven into flight. At last his army was scattered, and he was forced to hide himself in the woods and in lonely places among the mountains.

One rainy day, Bruce lay on the ground under a rude shed, listening to the patter of the drops on the roof above him. He was tired and sick at heart, and ready to give up all hope. It seemed to him that there was no use for him to try to do anything more.

 Habit points from *Laying Down the Rails*

As he lay thinking, he saw a spider over his head, making ready to weave her web. He watched her as she toiled slowly and with great care. Six times she tried to throw her frail thread from one beam to another, and six times it fell short.

"Poor thing!" said Bruce: "you, too, know what it is to fail."

But the spider did not lose hope with the sixth failure. With still more care, she made ready to try for the seventh time. Bruce almost forgot his own troubles as he watched her swing herself out upon the slender line. Would she fail again? No! The thread was carried safely to the beam, and fastened there.

"I, too, will try a seventh time!" cried Bruce.

He arose and called his men together. He told them of his plans, and sent them out with messages of cheer to his disheartened people. Soon there was an army of brave Scotchmen around him. Another battle was fought, and the King of England was glad to go back into his own country.

I have heard it said, that, after that day, no one by the name of Bruce would ever hurt a spider. The lesson which the little creature had taught the king was never forgotten.

Lesson 5

Discuss point five and the quotation together.

> *"Although the world is full of suffering, it is full also of the overcoming of it."* — *Helen Keller*

 5. When you focus on your comfort level, you are learning to concentrate on self instead of others.

Activity: Thinking of someone else when you are tempted to dwell on your own hurt is a great way to show Fortitude. Let your children think of an action they could take to help put others in the forefront of their minds the next time they want to dwell on their troubles. Practice that action. Suggestions: write an email or letter; write encouraging notes to friends, classmates, siblings; draw pictures to give away; pray for someone; help with a household responsibility.

Lesson 6

Talk over point ten, then read and discuss the poem, "If."

 10. Concentrate on your own duties and other people's rights, rather than your own rights and other people's duties.

If
by Rudyard Kipling

If you can keep your head when all about you
    Are losing theirs and blaming it on you;
If you can trust yourself when all men doubt you,
    But make allowance for their doubting too:
If you can wait and not be tired by waiting,
    Or, being lied about, don't deal in lies,
Or being hated don't give way to hating,
    And yet don't look too good, nor talk too wise;

4. A child who concentrates on physical discomfort is likely to grow up into an adult who obsesses about physical sensations and misses out on the joy of living.

6. Children with physical ailments should not be excluded and can benefit most from this training.

7. Be careful not to turn your child's thoughts to his physical ailments.

8. Don't intentionally inflict hardness on your child in order to "train him in fortitude"; simply redirect his thoughts away from physical discomfort when it occurs.

9. Be watchful for anything that might actually be dangerous or harmful to your child and deal with it in a calm manner.

If you can dream—and not make dreams your master;
　　If you can think—and not make thoughts your aim,
If you can meet with Triumph and Disaster
　　And treat those two impostors just the same:
If you can bear to hear the truth you've spoken
　　Twisted by knaves to make a trap for fools,
Or watch the things you gave your life to, broken,
　　And stoop and build 'em up with worn-out tools;

If you can make one heap of all your winnings
　　And risk it on one turn of pitch-and-toss,
And lose, and start again at your beginnings,
　　And never breathe a word about your loss:
If you can force your heart and nerve and sinew
　　To serve your turn long after they are gone,
And so hold on when there is nothing in you
　　Except the Will which says to them: "Hold on!"

If you can talk with crowds and keep your virtue,
　　Or walk with Kings—nor lose the common touch,
If neither foes nor loving friends can hurt you,
　　If all men count with you, but none too much:
If you can fill the unforgiving minute
　　With sixty seconds' worth of distance run,
Yours is the Earth and everything that's in it,
　　And—which is more—you'll be a Man, my son!

📖 *11. Pray for your child to have a servant's heart, then encourage that attitude with your actions.*

📖 *12. Use stirring stories and examples of fortitude to motivate your child's determination in the right direction.*

Lesson 7

Read and discuss the quotation and the story.

> *"Patience serves as a protection against wrongs as clothes do against cold. For if you put on more clothes as the cold increases, it will have no power to hurt you. So in like manner you must grow in patience when you meet with great wrongs, and they will then be powerless to vex your mind." — Leonardo da Vinci*

Cinderella
from *Fairy Stories and Fables* by James Baldwin

A very long time ago there lived a fair young girl with her father and mother in a beautiful home in the city. She was as happy as she was good, and she had all that a heart could wish. But, by and by, a sad day came, and then many sad days. Her mother fell sick and died; and then, some time after, her father married again, for he said that his daughter must have some one to take care of her.

After that everything went wrong. The new mother was very cross and unkind; and she had two daughters of her own who were as cross and unkind as herself. They were harsh and cruel to our fair young girl and made her do all the hard work about the house.

She swept the floors and scrubbed the stairs and washed the dishes and cleaned the grates, while her two sisters sat in the parlor or lay asleep on their soft beds. They slept in fine rooms where there were long looking-glasses in which they could see themselves from head to foot; but she was sent to lie on an old pile of straw in the attic where there was only one chair, and no looking-glass at all.

When her day's work was done, they did not allow her to come into the parlor, but made her sit in the chimney corner in the kitchen among the ashes and cinders. This is why they nicknamed her Cinderella, or the cinder maid. But, for all her shabby clothes, she was handsomer by half than they could ever be.

Now it happened that the King's son gave a ball, and he invited all the fine rich people in the city to come to it. Of course, Cinderella's sisters were to go; and they were very proud and happy, for they thought that perhaps the Prince would dance with them. As for Cinderella, it only meant more work for her; she must help her sisters get their fine dresses ready, and she must iron their laces and ribbons, and starch their linen, and put their ruffles in order. For days and days they talked of nothing but clothes.

"I am going to wear my blue velvet dress, and trim it with point lace," said the elder.

"And I am going to wear my pink satin, with diamonds and pearls," said the younger.

And then they began to quarrel; and they would have fought, I do believe, if Cinderella had not tried to make peace between them.

In the evening, while she was helping them with their hair, the elder said:

"Cinderella, don't you wish you were going to the ball to-night?"

"Ah, you are only laughing at me," she said. "It is not for me to go to so fine a place as that."

"You are right," said her sister. "Folks would think it very funny to see such a creature as you at a ball. The best place for you is among the ashes."

The sisters had laced themselves very tightly, for they wanted to look thin and slender; and they had eaten scarcely anything for two days. It is no wonder, then, that they were more ill-tempered that night than they had been before; and they scolded and fretted and frowned until there was no getting along with them at all. But Cinderella was as sweet and kind as ever, and seemed to take all the more pains to make them look handsome.

At last the coach stopped at the door; they hurried out, and climbed into it; and then they were whirled away to the ball.

As for Cinderella, she sat down by the kitchen fire and cried.

All at once a fairy stood before her and asked her what was the matter.

"I wish I could—I wish I could—" and that was all that Cinderella could say for weeping and sobbing.

"I know," said the fairy. "You want to go to the ball, don't you?"

"Y-yes," cried Cinderella; and then she sobbed harder than ever.

"Well," said the fairy, "I know you are a good girl, and I think we can manage it." Then she said, "Run into the garden and fetch me a pumpkin."

Cinderella did not stop to ask why, but ran out and soon brought in the finest pumpkin that she could find. The fairy scooped out the inside of it, and then struck it with her wand.

What a strange thing happened then! Before you could snap your fingers, the pumpkin was changed into a fine coach gilded all over and lined with red satin.

"Now fetch me the mouse trap from the pantry," said the fairy.

Cinderella did so; there were six fat mice in it. The fairy lifted the trap door, and, as the mice came out one by one, she touched them with her wand. You would have laughed to see how quickly they were changed into fine black horses.

"But what shall we do for a coachman, my Cinderella?" said the fairy.

"Maybe there is a rat in the rat trap," said Cinderella. "We might make a coachman of him."

"You are right," said the fairy; "go and see!"

Cinderella soon brought the rat trap, and in it there were three big rats. The fairy chose the finest one among them and touched him with her wand; and, quick as a flash, he became the fattest, jolliest coachman that you ever saw.

"Now, go into the garden," said the fairy, "and you will find six gray lizards behind the watering pot. Bring them to me."

She had no sooner done so than the fairy touched them with her wand and turned them into six foot-men, who stood in waiting behind the coach as if they had been footmen all their lives.

"Now then, my Cinderella," said the fairy, "now you can go to the ball."

"What! In these clothes?" said Cinderella; and she looked down at her ragged frock and began to sob again.

The fairy laughed, and touched her with her wand. You should have seen what happened then. Her clothes were turned into the finest cloth of gold and silver, all beset with rich jewels; and on her feet were glass slippers, the prettiest that ever were seen.

"Now, my Cinderella," said the fairy, "you must be off at once. But remember that if you stay a moment after midnight, your carriage will be a pumpkin again, and your coachman a rat, and your horses mice, and your footmen lizards, and yourself a ragged little cinder maid."

Then Cinderella stepped into her coach, the coachman cracked his whip, and away she was whirled to the ball.

Somebody had told the King's son that a beautiful Princess whom nobody knew was coming; and so, when the coach stopped at the palace door, there he was, ready to help her out. He led her into the hall, and all the fine people who were there stood aside to let her pass. Nobody could help looking at her. "Ha! how handsome she is! Ha! how handsome she is!" said one to another.

The King himself, old as he was, whispered to the Queen that he had never seen so fair a maiden; and all the ladies were busy looking at her clothes and planning how they would make theirs after the same pattern. Then the music struck up, and the King's son led her out to dance with him; and she danced with so much modesty and grace that everybody thought her more lovely than before.

By and by a fine supper was served, but the young Prince could not eat a mouthful, he was so busy thinking of her. Cinderella went and sat down by her sisters, and was very civil and kind to them; and this made them proud and glad, for they did not know her, and they thought it a grand thing to be noticed by so fine a lady.

While she was talking to them she heard the clock strike a quarter to twelve, and she remembered what the fairy had told her about staying till midnight. So she made haste to bid the King and Queen good night, and then, getting into her coach, she was driven home.

She met the fairy at the door and thanked her for her kindness; and the good fairy told her that she might go the next night to the Queen's ball, to which the Prince had invited her.

A few minutes later, the two sisters came home and found Cinderella sitting in the chimney corner, rubbing her eyes and seeming to be very sleepy.

"Ah, how long you have stayed!" she said.

"Well, if you had been there you would have stayed as long," said one of the sisters. "The prettiest Princess that you ever saw was there; and she talked with us and gave us bonbons."

"Who was she?" asked Cinderella.

"That's just what everybody would like to know," said the elder, whose name was Charlotte.

"Yes, the King's son would give the world to know who she is," said the younger, whose name was Caroline.

"I wish I could see her," said Cinderella. "Oh, dear Miss Charlotte, won't you let me go to-morrow? And, Miss Caroline, won't you lend me your yellow dress to wear?"

"What, lend my yellow dress to a cinder maid!" cried Caroline. "I'm not so foolish as that!" And the two sisters went proudly to their rooms.

The next night came, and the two sisters were at the ball, and so was Cinderella; and everybody thought her more beautiful than before. "Now remember twelve o'clock," were the fairy's last words when she started.

The young Prince was very kind to her, and time flew fast. The dancing was delightful, and the supper was fine, and nobody thought of being tired. But, before she had stayed half as long as she wished, Cinderella heard the clock begin to strike twelve. She rose up and ran from the room like a wild deer. The Prince followed her; but when he reached the street he saw nobody there but a ragged little cinder girl whom he would not have touched for the world.

Cinderella reached home, tired, frightened, and cold, without carriage, coachman, or footman; nothing was left of all her finery but one of her little glass slippers; the other she had dropped in the King's hall as she was running away.

When the two sisters came home, Cinderella asked them if they had had a good time at the ball, and if the pretty Princess had been there.

"Yes," they told her; "but when it struck twelve she ran away without bidding anybody good night; and she dropped one of her little glass slippers in the hall—the prettiest slipper that anybody ever saw. The King's son picked it up and put it into his pocket, as though it was the rarest treasure in the world. But nobody could find out which way the Princess went."

Cinderella climbed up the stairs to her wretched bed in the attic; and the next day she was at work, sweeping and scrubbing, as hard as ever.

And now, what do you think happened next? The King's son sent men with trumpets all through the land to invite every young lady to try the little glass slipper; and he declared that he would marry the one whose foot the slipper would just fit.

Of course, hundreds and hundreds of young ladies tried it; but their feet were ever and ever so much too big. You would have laughed to see the two sisters try it, and to hear their sighs when they had to give it up. Cinderella was very much amused, for she knew all the time that it was her slipper.

"Let me see if it will fit me," she said at last.

"What, you? Bah!" cried Charlotte, laughing.

"Go into the kitchen and clean the grates," said Caroline; and both of them tried to keep her from touching the slipper.

But the man who had been sent with the slipper said that he had orders to let every maiden in the land make the trial. So Cinderella sat down on a three-legged stool, and he put the slipper on her foot, and it fitted her as if it had been made of wax. And then she drew from her pocket the other slipper, and put it on her other foot.

At the same moment, in came the fairy with her wand; and she touched Cinderella, and she was no longer a cinder maid but a beautiful young lady clad in silk and satin.

And now the two sisters found that she was the pretty Princess whom they had seen at the ball; and they threw themselves at her feet to ask pardon for the unkind way in which they had treated her. She lifted them up kindly, and said that she forgave them, and wished them always to love her.

Some time afterwards, the young Prince and Cinderella were married; and they lived together happily for many, many years. As for the two sisters, Cinderella gave them rooms in the palace; and they left off their cross, ugly ways, and by and by became the wives of two rich dukes who were friends of the Prince.

Lesson 8

Read and discuss the quotation below.

> *"Character cannot be developed in ease and quiet. Only through experience of trial and suffering can the soul be strengthened, ambition inspired, and success achieved."*
> — *Helen Keller*

Read Job chapter 2. With all the awful calamities that came upon Job, he did not sin in what he said. He asked his wife, "Should we accept good from God, and not trouble?"

Lesson 9

Fortitude includes the element of standing against temptation. If you've never had to deny yourself as a child, you'll have a hard time saying No later in life when faced with greater temptation. Read and discuss the poem, "Our Heroes."

Our Heroes
by Phoebe Cary

Here's a hand to the boy who has courage
    To do what he knows to be right;
When he falls in the way of temptation,
    He has a hard battle to fight.
Who strives against self and his comrades
    Will find a most powerful foe;
All honor to him if he conquers—
    A cheer for the boy who says "No!"

There's many a battle fought daily
    The world knows nothing about;
There's many a brave little soldier
    Whose strength puts a legion to rout.
And he who fights sin single-handed
    Is more of a hero, I say,
Than he who leads soldiers to battle,
    And conquers by arms in the fray.

Be steadfast, my boy, when you're tempted
    And do what you know to be right;
Stand firm by the colors of manhood,
    And you will overcome in the fight.
"The Right" be your battle-cry ever,
    In waging the warfare of life;
And God, who knows who are the heroes,
    Will give you the strength for the strife.

Lesson 10

There are those who persevere with a calling even through obstacles and feelings of inadequacies. Read and discuss the quotation, making sure the children know Reeve's story from successful actor to quadriplegic. Then read and discuss the story that follows.

"I think a hero is an ordinary individual who finds strength to persevere and endure in spite of overwhelming obstacles." — Christopher Reeve

The Cowherd Who Became a Poet
from *Fifty Famous People* by James Baldwin

You can read the hymn Caedmon wrote in Lesson 2 of Praise on page 405.

I

In England there was once a famous abbey, called Whitby. It was so close to the sea that those who lived in it could hear the waves forever beating against the shore. The land around it was rugged, with only a few fields in the midst of a vast forest.

In those far-off days, an abbey was half church, half castle. It was a place where good people, and timid, helpless people could find shelter in time of war. There they might live in peace and safety while all the country round was overrun by rude and barbarous men.

One cold night in winter the serving men of the abbey were gathered in the great kitchen. They were sitting around the fire and trying to keep themselves warm.

Out of doors the wind was blowing. The men heard it as it whistled through the trees and rattled the doors of the abbey. They drew up closer to the fire and felt thankful that they were safe from the raging storm.

"Who will sing us a song?" said the master woodman as he threw a fresh log upon the fire.

"Yes, a song! a song!" shouted some of the others. "Let us have a good old song that will help to keep us warm."

"We can all be minstrels tonight," said the chief cook. "Suppose we each sing a song in turn. What say you?"

"Agreed! agreed!" cried the others. "And the cook shall begin."

The woodman stirred the fire until the flames leaped high and the sparks flew out of the roof hole. Then the chief cook began his song. He sang of war, and of bold rough deeds, and of love and sorrow.

After him the other men were called, one by one; and each in turn sang his favorite song. The woodman sang of the wild forest; the plowman sang of the fields; the shepherd sang of his sheep; and those who listened forgot about the storm and the cold weather.

But in the corner, almost hidden from his fellows, one poor man was sitting who did not enjoy the singing. It was Caedmon, the cowherd.

"What shall I do when it comes my turn?" he said to himself. "I do not know any song. My voice is harsh and I cannot sing."

So he sat there trembling and afraid; for he was a timid, bashful man and did not like to be noticed.

At last, just as the blacksmith was in the midst of a stirring song, he rose quietly and went out into the darkness. He went across the narrow yard to the sheds where the cattle were kept in stormy weather.

"The gentle cows will not ask a song of me," said the poor man. He soon found a warm corner, and there he lay down, covering himself with the straw.

Inside of the great kitchen, beside the fire, the men were shouting and laughing; for the blacksmith had finished his song, and it was very pleasing.

"Who is next?" asked the woodman.

"Caedmon, the keeper of the cows," answered the chief cook.

"Yes, Caedmon! Caedmon!" all shouted together. "A song from Caedmon!" But when they looked, they saw that his seat was vacant.

"The poor, timid fellow!" said the blacksmith. "He was afraid and has slipped away from us."

II

In his safe, warm place in the straw, Caedmon soon fell asleep. All around him were the cows of the abbey, some chewing their cuds, and others like their master quietly sleeping. The singing in the kitchen was ended, the fire had burned low, and each man had gone to his place.

Then Caedmon had a strange dream. He thought that a wonderful light was shining around him. His eyes were dazzled by it. He rubbed them with his hands, and when they were quite open he thought that he saw a beautiful face looking down upon him, and that a gentle voice said,—

"Caedmon, sing for me."

At first he was so bewildered that he could not answer. Then he heard the voice again.

"Caedmon, sing something."

"Oh, I cannot sing," answered the poor man. "I do not know any song; and my voice is harsh and unpleasant. It was for this reason that I left my fellows in the abbey kitchen and came here to be alone."

"But you must sing," said the voice. "You must sing."

"What shall I sing?" he asked.

"Sing of the creation," was the answer.

Then Caedmon, with only the cows as his hearers, opened his mouth and began to sing. He sang of the beginning of things; how the world was made; how the sun and moon came into being; how the land rose from the water; how the birds and the beasts were given life.

All through the night he sat among the abbey cows, and sang his wonderful song. When the stable boys and shepherds came out in the morning, they heard him singing; and they were so amazed that they stood still in the drifted snow and listened with open mouths.

At length, others of the servants heard him, and were entranced by his wonderful song. And one ran quickly and told the good abbess, or mistress of the abbey, what strange thing had happened.

"Bring the cowherd hither, that I and those who are with me may hear him," said she.

So Caedmon was led into the great hall of the abbey. And all of the sweet-faced sisters and other women of the place listened while he sang again the wonderful song of the creation.

"Surely," said the abbess, "this is a poem, most sweet, most true, most beautiful. It must be written down so that people in other places and in other times may hear it read and sung."

So she called her clerk, who was a scholar, and bade him write the song, word for word, as it came from Caedmon's lips. And this he did.

Such was the way in which the first true English poem was written. And Caedmon, the poor cowherd of the abbey, was the first great poet of England.

Lesson 11

Sometimes when we face hardship or death and accept it, we deal with it more serenely and with steadfast purpose.

Read Esther chapter 4. Esther had been notified of Haman's plot and exhorted by her Uncle Mordecai to use her position as queen to change matters for her people. Esther was afraid but was willing to face death in order to obtain the king's help.

Lesson 12

Have a Parent Share moment to share a story from your life or tell about a person who exemplifies Fortitude, then discuss the quotation below.

"Courage and perseverance have a magical talisman, before which difficulties disappear and obstacles vanish into air." — *John Quincy Adams*

Finish up with any other discussion, ideas, or celebration your family enjoys. Keep up this habit while going forth to concentrate on a new one.

Health

*Taking good care of your body,
through nutrition, hygiene, exercise, and rest*

Parent Prep

Read detailed thoughts about Health on pages 127–129 of *Laying Down the Rails* and skim the lessons below.

♦ Goals for this Habit (and steps to get there)

_____

_____

_____

♦ A Person or Story from My Life that Demonstrates this Habit

_____

_____

_____

♦ Additional Stories, Poems, Quotations, Bible Verses I Want to Use

_____

_____

_____

♦ Other Activities We Could Do to Practice this Habit

_____

_____

_____

Charlotte wrote directly to young people about Health in Volume 4, Book 1, pages 11–20.

♦ Celebration Ideas

_____

_____

_____

Lesson 1

Read the definition and discuss Health. Share with the children any goals you've identified for this habit (for instance, "We will have at least one hour of physical activity a day."). Also get their input on changes they think need to be made.

Read the Biblical principle found in 3 John verse 2 from your preferred version of the Bible.

1. Family meals are a great time to teach good nutrition and encourage good eating habits.

 2. Don't allow your child unhealthy indulgences.

Health allows us to be useful, productive citizens in our world and in God's kingdom.

Lesson 2

Discuss point three, giving examples of Health habits that older children become responsible for: brushing and flossing teeth, hair care, and food choices. Read and discuss the poem below.

 3. As you get older, health becomes your own responsibility.

Good and Bad Children
by Robert Louis Stevenson

Children, you are very little,
And your bones are very brittle;
If you would grow great and stately,
You must try to walk sedately.

You must still be bright and quiet,
And content with simple diet;
And remain, through all bewild'ring,
Innocent and honest children.

Happy hearts and happy faces,
Happy play in grassy places—
That was how in ancient ages,
Children grew to kings and sages.

But the unkind and the unruly,
And the sort who eat unduly,
They must never hope for glory—
Theirs is quite a different story!

Cruel children, crying babies,
All grow up as geese and gabies,
Hated, as their age increases,
By their nephews and their nieces.

Lesson 3

Talk about point four, giving the opposite statement also: Good Health habits now can reap a thriving body in future years. Read and discuss the Shakespeare quotation and the story, "The Old Man and the King."

"Our bodies are our gardens—our wills are our gardeners." — *William Shakespeare*

 4. Poor health habits now will reap a failing body in future years.

 Habit points from *Laying Down the Rails*

The Old Man and the King
from *Harper's Third Reader*, edited by James Baldwin

A very old man was one day planting some fig trees in his garden, when the king, who was passing that way, stopped to talk with him.

"Why is it," said the king, "that a man of your age must toil in this way? If you had made good use of the morning hours of your life you would not need to work so hard now in the evening of your days."

"Good king," said the man, "the early days of my life were well spent, for I left no duty undone; and now, in the evening of my life, I shall still do what my hands find to do, hoping that I shall never be a burden to the world."

"How old are you, kind father?" asked the king.

"A hundred years," answered the man.

"What!" cried the king, "a hundred years old, and still planting trees? Surely, you do not hope ever to enjoy the fruit of your labor!"

"Great king," said the silver-haired man, "I do hope so. If God wills it, I may even eat of the fruit of these very trees; if not, then my children will be here to enjoy it. Did not my forefathers plant trees for me, and shall I not do the same for my children and grandchildren?"

The king was pleased with the man's honest words, and he said: "Well, my good old friend, if, indeed, you do live to see these trees bearing fruit, let me know about it." With these words he left the old man and went on his way.

Many years after this the king sat in his palace, weary and careworn, and feeling that there was little to hope for in the days that were coming. As he looked out of the window he saw a man, bent with age, standing near the gate, with a basket on his arm, and he told the servants to bring him in.

"What is it that you wish, old man?" asked the king.

"Good king," answered the man, "you have not forgotten the talk which you once had with a very old man planting some trees. You asked him that, if ever he should gather the fruit, he would let you know. I am that old man, and I have brought you the first fruit of those very trees. May it please you to take it as a humble token of my good will towards you."

The king was much pleased with the wisdom and goodness of the old man. He thanked him kindly for the fruit, and told him to wait a little while until it should be taken from the basket. When the basket was given back to its owner it was full of gold, which the king begged him to take as a token of his esteem.

Lesson 4

Read and discuss the quotation.

> *"The greatest wealth is health."* — *Virgil*

Activity: Gather library books or research and purchase good books on Health for the different ages and genders of your children. Take some time to practice problem areas of Health: it could be brushing teeth, drinking plenty of water, getting more exercise, or having rest time in the afternoon.

Lesson 5

God knows we have physical needs and provides for them. First Timothy 6:6–8 talks about being content with food and clothing. We don't have to be over zealous and spend lots of time and money in our pursuit of Health.

Read 1 Kings chapter 17. God used ravens and a widow to give food and water to Elijah during a drought.

Lesson 6

Supervised outdoor play with neighboring children is an easy way to get physical exercise every day. Read the poem, "The Echoing Green."

The Echoing Green
by William Blake

The sun does arise,
And make happy the skies;
The merry bells ring
To welcome the spring;
The skylark and thrush,
The birds of the bush,
Sing louder around
To the bells' cheerful sound,
While our sports shall be seen
On the echoing green.

Old John with white hair,
Does laugh away care,
Sitting under the oak,
Among the old folk.
They laugh at our play,
And soon they all say:
'Such, such were the joys
When we all, girls and boys,
In our youth time were seen
On the echoing green.'

Till the little ones, weary,
No more can be merry;
The sun does descend,
And our sports have an end.
Round the laps of their mothers
Many sisters and brothers,
Like birds in their nest,
Are ready for rest,
And sport no more seen
On the darkening green.

Lesson 7

Have a Parent Share moment to share a story from your life or tell about a person who exemplifies the habit of Health, then read and discuss the quotation below.

"Lack of activity destroys the good condition of every human being, while movement and methodical physical exercise save it and preserve it." — *Plato*

Lesson 8

A body in good health is at the ready when an emergency requires physical action. Read and discuss "Margaret, The Fisher Girl."

Margaret, The Fisher Girl
from *Harper's Third Reader,* edited by James Baldwin

There is a little village on the north coast of Scotland where all the men are fishermen. They live very quiet lives, and know but little about the rest of the world. When they come home with their loads of fish the women go down to the beach to meet the boats, and then carry the baskets filled with fish to the carts which are waiting higher up on the shore. The girls are as hardy and brave as the boys, and are taught to work outdoors as well as indoors.

Margaret was a brown-cheeked lass, much like the other girls of her age in the village. She lived with her poor mother in a little cottage which stood close by the sea, and she had never known any other life than that of toil. Yet she was cheerful and contented, and always happy when there was work for her to do.

One evening last summer every boat in the little village had gone to sea; for there were a great many fish at that season of the year, and the best time to take them was during the night. Not a man was left at home except three very old fishermen who were no longer able to do any hard work.

In the night there came up a strong south wind. It blew so hard, and the waves rolled so high, that the boats could not sail back home; but they found a safe shelter in a little harbor many miles farther north. When morning came the women and children in the village looked out upon a stormy sea. Great clouds of foam flew before the wind, dashed against the houses by the shore, and were carried even into the fields beyond; and the waves as they broke among the rocks seemed to shake the ground.

When the storm was at its highest, a ship was seen coming in from the sea, and drifting towards some rocks which lay just outside of the bay. There was no help for her; the storm drove her onward; she soon struck.

As she lay helpless upon the rocks, the waves dashed over her decks, and every moment it seemed as if they would break her to pieces. Her crew were seen holding on to the masts and ropes. There was no boat to send to their aid, and the women and children who stood near the shore expected to see the vessel broken up and the men drowned before their eyes.

"Will she last until noon?" cried Margaret. "If I thought she would hang together so long, I'd run and send the lifeboat."

"Ah, my lass," said one of the old men, "you could never cross the burn after such a storm as this."

Four miles farther south there was a village where a lifeboat was kept, and there were men there whose duty it was to help those who were in danger along the coast. Halfway to that village there was a stream, usually shallow, which ran into the sea and over which was a rude bridge. It was this stream, or burn, as he called it, which the old man said she could never cross.

"I'll away, and try it, at least!" said Margaret. Across the fields she ran for a mile, in the face of the storm. The second mile was still harder, for her way was close to the shore. More than once the waves almost dragged her off her feet.

When she came to the burn she felt for a moment like giving up. The little bridge had been washed away. There was no guessing how deep the stream was, for the water was very swift and the bottom could not be seen. In she plunged. The water was up to her arms. Once she stumbled and fell, but was quickly on her feet again. Then the water grew deeper. Reaching out her arms, Margaret battled with the swift stream, and, half wading, half swimming, she at last reached the hard ground.

Two miles farther, through wind and driving rain she fought her way. She was faint and out of breath when she reached the house where the keeper of the lifeboat lived.

"The ship! On the Letch rocks!"—that was all that she could say, yet she was understood.

"Here, wife, take care of the lass!" cried the man, and, followed by his fellow-helpers, he ran to his boat. Poor, brave Margaret! Her part of the work was done, and she fainted quite away in the arms of the sailor's wife. But the lifeboat was soon floating upon the waves; out upon the stormy sea it was driven by the strong oars of the sailor-men; it reached the ship in time, and carried all the crew in safety to the shore.

Lesson 9

Rest is part of a healthy lifestyle.

Read Psalm 127. Then discuss the many word pictures of rest in the Shakespeare quotation below.

"Sleep that knits up the ravelled sleeve of care,
The death of each day's life, sore labour's bath,
Balm of hurt minds, great nature's second course,
Chief nourisher in life's feast." — William Shakespeare

Lesson 10

Many bad habits can develop in the area of Health. Make sure your children understand *why* certain habits can ruin one's health, rather than just being told what to do and not to do. Give your children sound principles, not just opinions, so they will be well equipped to make good decisions in future situations. Read and discuss the story about "Sir Walter Raleigh."

Sir Walter Raleigh
adapted from *Fifty Famous Stories Retold* by James Baldwin

Sir Walter Raleigh and Sir Humphrey Gilbert about whom I have already told you, were half-brothers.

When Sir Humphrey made his first voyage to America, Sir Walter was with him. After that, Sir Walter tried several times to send men to this country to make a settlement.

But those whom he sent found only great forests, and wild beasts, and savage Indians. Some of them went back to England; some of them died for want of food; and some of them were lost in the woods. At last Sir Walter gave up trying to get people to come to America.

But he found two things in this country which the people of England knew very little about. One was the potato, the other was tobacco.

If you should ever go to Ireland, you may be shown the place where Sir Walter planted the few potatoes which he carried over from America. He told his friends how the Indians used them for food; and he proved that they would grow in the Old World as well as in the New.

Sir Walter had seen the Indians smoking the leaves of the tobacco plant. He thought that he would do the same, and he carried some of the leaves to England. Englishmen had never used tobacco before that time; and all who saw Sir Walter puffing away at a roll of leaves thought that it was a strange sight.

One day as he was sitting in his chair and smoking, his servant came into the room. The man saw the smoke curling over his master's head, and he thought that he was on fire.

He ran out for some water. He found a pail that was quite full. He hurried back, and threw the water into Sir Walter's face. Of course the fire was all put out.

After that a great many men learned to smoke. And now tobacco is used in all countries of the world. It would have been well if Sir Walter Raleigh had let it alone.

Lesson 11

Continue to encourage one another as you train for Health.

Activity: Play some fun active games like any variation of tag, jump rope, hopscotch, musical chairs, water balloon fight, or balloon volleyball.

Lesson 12

Finish up with any other discussion, ideas, or celebration your family enjoys. Keep up this habit while going forth to concentrate on a new one.

Managing One's Own Body

*Knowing where one's body parts are in space
and being able to use them to best advantage*

Parent Prep

Read detailed thoughts about Managing One's Own Body on pages 129–133 of *Laying Down the Rails* and skim the lessons below.

♦ Goals for this Habit (and steps to get there)

_____

_____

_____

♦ A Person or Story from My Life that Demonstrates this Habit

_____

_____

_____

♦ Additional Stories, Poems, Quotations, Bible Verses I Want to Use

_____

_____

_____

Sticking together to work on one habit at a time helps the family focus and strengthen each other.

♦ Other Activities We Could Do to Practice this Habit

_____

_____

_____

♦ Celebration Ideas

_____

_____

_____

Lesson 1

Read the definition and discuss Managing One's Own Body. Share with the children any goals you've identified for this habit (for instance, "We will practice Swedish drill for 10 minutes a day."). Also get their input on changes they think need to be made.

Read the Biblical principle found in 1 Corinthians 9:24–27 from your preferred version of the Bible. Paul used the analogy of athletics in this passage. We should make our bodies our servants and not our masters.

Lesson 2

Discuss point one and come up with a plan for including such activities in your week, if you don't already.

 1. **Dancing, calisthenics, and daily physical exercise will help you become familiar with your body's movements and place in the space around you.**

Read Judges 16:21–31. Even though blind, Samson was able to situate himself to best overcome his enemies.

Lesson 3

Talk over point three. We are best able to be useful, to seize opportunities, and to show temperance or fortitude when our physical bodies have been trained to respond to our wishes. Read and discuss the story of "Grace Darling."

 3. **Physical training can help support moral training.**

2. Swedish drill can be adapted for all ages.

See page 342 for a description of Swedish Drill.

Grace Darling
from *Fifty Famous Stories Retold* by James Baldwin

It was a dark September morning. There was a storm at sea. A ship had been driven on a low rock off the shores of the Farne Islands. It had been broken in two by the waves, and half of it had been washed away. The other half lay yet on the rock, and those of the crew who were still alive were clinging to it. But the waves were dashing over it, and in a little while it too would be carried to the bottom.

Could any one save the poor, half-drowned men who were there?

On one of the islands was a lighthouse; and there, all through that stormy night, Grace Darling had listened to the storm.

Grace was the daughter of the lighthouse keeper, and she had lived by the sea as long as she could remember.

In the darkness of the night, above the noise of the winds and waves, she heard screams and wild cries. When daylight came, she could see the wreck, a mile away, with the angry waters all around it. She could see the men clinging to the masts.

"We must try to save them!" she cried. "Let us go out in the boat at once!"

"It is of no use, Grace," said her father. "We cannot reach them."

He was an old man, and he knew the force of the mighty waves.

"We cannot stay here and see them die," said Grace. "We must at least try to save them."

Her father could not say, "No."

In a few minutes they were ready. They set off in the heavy lighthouse boat. Grace pulled one oar, and her father the other, and they made straight toward the wreck. But it was hard rowing against such a sea, and it seemed as though they would never reach the place.

At last they were close to the rock, and now they were in greater danger than before. The fierce waves broke against the boat, and it would have been dashed in pieces, had it not been for the strength and skill of the brave girl.

But after many trials, Grace's father climbed upon the wreck, while Grace herself

 Habit points from *Laying Down the Rails*

held the boat. Then one by one the worn-out crew were helped on board. It was all that the girl could do to keep the frail boat from being drifted away, or broken upon the sharp edges of the rock.

Then her father clambered back into his place. Strong hands grasped the oars, and by and by all were safe in the lighthouse. There Grace proved to be no less tender as a nurse than she had been brave as a sailor. She cared most kindly for the ship-wrecked men until the storm had died away and they were strong enough to go to their own homes.

All this happened a long time ago, but the name of Grace Darling will never be forgotten. She lies buried now in a little churchyard by the sea, not far from her old home. Every year many people go there to see her grave; and there a monument has been placed in honor of the brave girl. It is not a large monument, but it is one that speaks of the noble deed which made Grace Darling famous. It is a figure carved in stone of a woman lying at rest, with a boat's oar held fast in her right hand.

Lesson 4

Talk about point four.

 4. Just as our bodies adjust to repeated physical actions, so our minds respond to repeated actions or thoughts and form habits.

Activity: Go to a playground and play a game of "Follow the Leader" where the leader leads the family through the different activities the playground offers: monkey bars, slide, swing, running up stairs, etc. You can add jumping jacks, push ups or lunges in between each equipment challenge. You could also just play "Follow the Leader" at home and lead the family through different exercises as you walk around the house or yard, stopping at certain areas to do a set: jumping jacks, push ups (these can be done against a wall for beginners), squats, or bench dips.

Lesson 5

We are all uniquely made and need to understand our own physical capabilities and limitations. Read and discuss how this principle is illustrated in the poem, "The Little Elf-man."

The Little Elf-man
by John Kendrick Bangs

I met a little Elf-man once,
   Down where the lilies blow.
I asked him why he was so small,
   And why he didn't grow.

He slightly frowned, and with his eye
   He looked me through and through—
"I'm quite as big for me," said he,
   "As you are big for you!"

Lesson 6

Have a Parent Share moment to share a story from your life or tell about a person who exemplifies Managing One's Own Body, then read and discuss the quotation below.

"Walking is the best possible exercise. Habituate yourself to walk very far." —
Thomas Jefferson

Lesson 7

Dexterity, as opposed to clumsiness, can be practiced and will be useful for accomplishments.

Read Nehemiah chapter 4. Because of threats of attacks, the men had to build the wall and alertly be prepared for battle at any moment. Some men had to carry materials while simultaneously holding weapons.

Lesson 8

Understand what your body needs. In this story, "How Billy Goes Coasting," the children knew they needed to walk uphill periodically in order to keep warm in the winter weather.

How Billy Goes Coasting
from *Harper's Third Reader*, edited by James Baldwin

Billy is a gray horse belonging to a family in a small country town. When the boys and girls go out coasting he goes with them to take part in the sport—that is, he does the work while the children have the fun.

The boys have a long double sled which carries a good many of them at once. It is fine fun to coast down the long hill upon it, but it is hard work to drag it up again. So they harness Billy to the sled and he drags it up for them.

Sometimes the boys think that they will ride up the hill as well as down, and draw some of the single sleds up with them. But they usually walk up, because the exercise keeps them warm.

When they reach the top they throw the reins on Billy's back, and he jogs down to the foot of the hill and waits for them to come down again. He seems to enjoy the sport as much as any of them, but he does not like too heavy a load.

Once, when he had drawn a large number of children up the hill—too many, he thought—and the boys had thrown the reins upon his back, he said, in his language, "You loaded me too heavily this time; the next time you may come up without my help!" and he trotted off to his stable.

Sometimes he takes a merry party of boys and girls upon the big double sled all about town. If the snow is deep the sled is quite sure to be upset a few times, but the children do not mind that, for the snow is soft, and Billy does not go fast, and no one is hurt.

The children are very kind to Billy, and he returns the kindness as well as he is able.

Lesson 9

Continue practicing this habit with good and encouraging attitudes.

Activity: Spend some time and effort investing in an active family class or sport. Tae Kwon Do, square dancing, calisthenics, or even swimming could be good choices. In place of a class, you could find a video that leads family-friendly exercises or teaches square dancing. Swedish drill can be learned and used at home or in a group environment. A description of Swedish drill is included below.

Swedish Drill (Drilling)
by Sonya Shafer
SimplyCharlotteMason.com

So many times as a homeschool parent I find it easy to ignore or at least minimize the importance of PE (Physical Education, or "gym class," as we called it when I went to school). Somehow I can't envision Charlotte Mason teaching the children how to play kick ball or dodge ball. (Not to mention that those games are a little difficult to do at home when you have only three or four children involved!) And I couldn't reconcile her beautiful educational philosophy with the notion of compelling children to do mindless repetitions, like twenty-five jumping jacks and fifty sit-ups.

Therefore, this whole idea of "drilling" (i.e., Swedish drill) that was used in her schools intrigued me, and I went on a hunt for more information. Well, the wonderful inter-library loan lady at my local library found me a gem: The Swedish Drill Teacher by M. H. Spalding, copyright 1910. This little 72-page book (which sold for six shillings in London) details the principles behind and methods of Swedish drill; and as I read about it, I was struck with how neatly it falls into step with Charlotte's philosophy of education.

For example, the exercises and movements were used with a view to improving "the general health of the body rather than towards muscular development." The drills were done outside whenever possible to allow for fresh air and deep breathing. The movements were done to command so the "pupils learn the power of quick and correct response to the command, and this involves concentration and quickness of thought, alertness of action, and effort of will. Since fresh commands for new and more complicated movements are continually being learnt, these qualities are always being more and more highly and acutely developed."

Those comments dovetail wonderfully with Charlotte's emphasis of a "serviceable body" as the goal of physical training (*School Education*, pp. 102, 103), her encouragement to spend lots of time outdoors (*Home Education*, p. 42), and the prominence she gave to the habits of full attention and mental alertness (*Home Education*, pp. 156, 185).

So what exactly is Swedish drill, you ask?

Swedish drill was a series of movements the students performed in response to the teacher's vocal instructions. The movements were performed slowly and gently (for the most part), with an emphasis on balance and complete muscle control. As students grew more proficient, the instructions progressed to more complicated postures or movements.

Movements centered around the arms bending and stretching, the arm and shoulder muscles, abdominal muscles, and legs muscles. Some jumping, marching, and running were also included, along with breathing exercises when needed to regulate after a strenuous exercise. Each drill session began with "introductory movements," similar to what we call "warming up."

The teachers would start with various fundamental positions in different combinations. For example, here are some

 ◆ Fundamental Arm positions: hands on hips, hands on shoulders, hands behind head with fingers lightly interlocked, arms extended (either up, down, out, or forward);

 ◆ Fundamental Foot positions: astride (legs parallel with shoulders but wider than shoulders), walk (a comfortable step in the direction indicated), lunge (a long step in the direction indicated);

♦ Fundamental Body positions: standing, sitting, lying, kneeling.

The instruction would be spoken once, with a pause for students to get a mental image of the position and how to move; then the "execution command" would be given (like "firm!" or "place!"), at which time the students would move. So the instruction "With feet astride, hands on hips (—pause—) firm!" would tell the students to place their hands on their hips while standing (with good posture, of course).

Simple arm instructions might be "Arms forward, sideways, and downward—stretch: 1, 2, 3" (with a change of position on each number).

After the students found those fundamental positions no longer a challenge, the teacher would start to mix things up a bit with variations. For example, our first instruction used above could be expanded from "with feet astride, hands on hips—firm!" to "Hips—firm! Feet astride—place: 1, 2! (Student would move one foot on each number spoken.) Feet together—place: 1, 2! Left foot forward—place! Feet change: 1, 2!" (On "1" the left foot is brought back; on "2" the right foot is moved forward.)

Or they could increase the complexity of arm movement instructions by having each arm do a different position. "Left arm upward, right arm forward—stretch!"

Next, they could combine arm and leg positions, such as "With left foot forward, right hand neck rest, left hand hips—firm! Feet and arms—change: 1, 2! (One "1" students come back to neutral position, and on "2" the positions of feet and arms are reversed.)

The possibilities for combinations are endless when you throw in heel raising, facing different sides of the room, toe standing, knee bending, "half" positions (doing the movement with one side of the body only, such as half kneel), knee raising, leg raising, bending or twisting at the waist, controlled jumping, and marching in patterns. If you'll pardon the comparison, the whole thing almost reminds me of a very advanced game of Simon Says.

The teacher was also encouraged to come up with some fun games and names for certain movements for the younger children (ages 6 to 8). For example, the "Do as I say, not as I do" game expected the children to listen carefully to the instructions and follow them even if the teacher took a different position. She might tell the children "Hips—firm!" but put her own hands behind her head. Or a fun balance movement would be "Taking off the shoe," for which each student would bend the knee up and stand on one foot while taking off his or her shoe and putting it on again. Small children would also get to do "giant marching" or "dwarf marching" and "bunny jumps."

There you have it: a quick overview of Swedish drill. I hope the explanation wasn't too confusing. It's hard to condense a 72-page book of instructions and physical movements.

Judging from the sample schedules, Charlotte's schools did drill for about 30 minutes at a time. You can be sure the drill teacher had thought through the combinations and sequence before attempting to lead the children for that length of time. Some of us would be challenged just to think up enough variations to occupy ten minutes if we were operating off the top of our heads! But as a quick diversion in the midst of lessons, it might prove to be an enjoyable spontaneous exercise.

Lesson 10

Finish up with any other discussion, ideas, or celebration your family enjoys. Keep up this habit while going forth to concentrate on a new one.

Music
Singing in tune

Parent Prep

Read detailed thoughts about Music on pages 133–135 of *Laying Down the Rails* and skim the lessons below.

♦ Goals for this Habit (and steps to get there)

_____

_____

_____

♦ A Person or Story from My Life that Demonstrates this Habit

_____

_____

_____

♦ Additional Stories, Poems, Quotations, Bible Verses I Want to Use

_____

_____

_____

♦ Other Activities We Could Do to Practice this Habit

_____

_____

_____

♦ Celebration Ideas

_____

_____

_____

Lesson 1

Read the definition and discuss Music. Share with the children any goals you've identified for this habit (for instance, "We will listen to music in the morning as we get ready for the day and in the van as we drive around doing errands."). Also get their input on changes they think need to be made.

Read the Biblical principle found in Ephesians 5:19 and 20 from your preferred version of the Bible. Music teaches, expresses emotion, and touches a person's heart and soul.

Lesson 2

Children love free expression with simple musical instruments. Read and enjoy the poem, "The Concert," then have a time of music, yourselves. If you don't have musical instruments, find objects around the house that emit different tones when struck with a wooden spoon, a hand, or a metal spoon. Have fun tapping along to various songs or rhymes.

The Concert
from *The Infant's Delight*

See how it rains! We cannot go
Our walk across the fields; and so,
Since Tom and Ettie Holmes are come,
And cousin Fred has brought his drum,
And some can sing, and others play,
We'll have a concert here today.
You, Tom, must in the middle stand,
And mark the time, with stick in hand;
You, brother Ben, the tongs must take,
For they will good triangles make;
Hal clicks the 'bones,' and Emmeline
Will beat her little tambourine,
And cousin Fred will drum away,
And Kate the concertina play.
All must attend to Tom; and mind
None play too fast, nor lag behind;
And then, I'm sure, we all shall see
How grand a concert this will be,
And say this is the wisest way
To spend this wet October day.

1. Surround your child with good music so he constantly hears musical sounds.

2. Some children may take to singing quite naturally, while others may require more training in music.

3. Provide carefully graduated exercises or lessons that teach musical tones and intervals.

Lesson 3

Music can lift your spirits.

Read 1 Samuel 16:14–23. Soothing music from a harp calmed Saul's troubled spirit.

Lesson 4

Talk about how music can be a gift to others. Read and discuss "The Arrow and the Song."

The Arrow and the Song
by Henry Wadsworth Longfellow

I shot an arrow into the air,
It fell to earth, I knew not where;
For, so swiftly it flew, the sight
Could not follow it in its flight.

Habit points from *Laying Down the Rails*

I breathed a song into the air,
It fell to earth, I knew not where;
For who has sight so keen and strong,
That it can follow the flight of song?

Long, long afterward, in an oak
I found the arrow, still unbroke;
And the song, from beginning to end,
I found again in the heart of a friend.

Lesson 5

Read and discuss the quotation below. Ask your children how they would define a "music bath."

"Take a music bath once or twice a week for a few seasons. You will find it is to the soul what a water bath is to the body." — *Oliver Wendell Holmes*

Activity: Watch the movie, *The Sound of Music*, or find a clip of the "Do Re Mi" song from that movie to see an example of Sol-fa. There are many familiar songs in this movie that are fun for the family to sing along to.

Lesson 6

Music can give expression to your feelings, which helps in the release of those feelings so they don't stay trapped inside. Read and discuss the poem, "King David."

King David
by Walter de la Mare

King David was a sorrowful man:
No cause for his sorrow had he;
And he called for the music of a hundred harps,
To ease his melancholy.

They played till they all fell silent:
Played—and play sweet did they;
But the sorrow that haunted the heart of King David
They could not charm away.

He rose; and in his garden
Walked by the moon alone,
A nightingale hidden in a cypress-tree
Jargoned on and on.

King David lifted his sad eyes
Into the dark-boughed tree—
"Tell me, thou little bird that singest,
Who taught my grief to thee?"

But the bird in no wise heeded
And the king in the cool of the moon
Hearkened to the nightingale's sorrowfulness,
Till all his own was gone.

Lesson 7

Each culture has its own distinct use of instrument and voice. The Israelites had their own sound also. There's a whole book of songs in the Bible (Psalms) and mention of singing or verses of songs throughout the Bible.

Read 2 Chronicles chapter 7. Music was a part of the ceremony at the dedication of the temple Solomon built.

Lesson 8

Some people have been blessed with a gift for music: writing, reading, playing, teaching, or singing. It is an ability that can be developed and used in service to God and others. Read and discuss the two poems below.

Piping Down the Valleys Wild
by William Blake

Piping down the valleys wild,
    Piping songs of pleasant glee,
On a cloud I saw a child,
    And he laughing said to me:

'Pipe a song about a lamb!'
    So I piped with merry cheer.
'Piper, pipe that song again.'
    So I piped: he wept to hear.

'Drop thy pipe, thy happy pipe;
    Sing thy songs of happy cheer.'
So I sung the same again,
    While he wept with joy to hear.

'Piper, sit thee down and write
    In a book, that all may read.'
So he vanished from my sight,
    And I plucked a hollow reed,

And I made a rural pen,
    And I stained the water clear,
And I wrote my happy songs
    Every child may joy to hear.

The Solitary Reaper
by William Wordsworth

Behold her, single in the field,
Yon solitary Highland Lass!
Reaping and singing by herself;
Stop here, or gently pass!
Alone she cuts and binds the grain,
And sings a melancholy strain;
O listen! for the Vale profound
Is overflowing with the sound.

No Nightingale did ever chaunt
More welcome notes to weary bands
Of travellers in some shady haunt,
Among Arabian sands:
A voice so thrilling ne'er was heard
In spring-time from the Cuckoo-bird,
Breaking the silence of the seas
Among the farthest Hebrides.

Will no one tell me what she sings?—
Perhaps the plaintive numbers flow
For old, unhappy, far-off things,
And battles long ago:
Or is it some more humble lay,
Familiar matter of to-day?
Some natural sorrow, loss, or pain,
That has been, and may be again?

Whate'er the theme, the Maiden sang
As if her song could have no ending;
I saw her singing at her work,
And o'er the sickle bending;—
I listen'd, motionless and still;
And, as I mounted up the hill,
The music in my heart I bore,
Long after it was heard no more.

Lesson 9

Read and discuss the quotation below.

"Alas for those that never sing,
But die with all their music in them!" — Oliver Wendell Homes

Activity: Hold a family sing-along. Let each child choose his or her favorite folk song, hymn, or praise song and let the whole family join in singing it together. Print copies of the words if the songs are unfamiliar. In place of a sing-along, you could let each child take a day for choosing the music to be listened to throughout that day.

Lesson 10

Even those without a special gift of music can practice and become better at staying in tune. Read and discuss the two poems.

The Poet's Song
by Alfred, Lord Tennyson

The rain had fallen, the Poet arose,
   He passed by the town, and out of the street,
A light wind blew from the gates of the sun,
   And waves of shadow went over the wheat,
And he set him down in a lonely place,
   And chanted a melody loud and sweet,
That made the wild-swan pause in her cloud,
   And the lark drop down at his feet.

The swallow stopt as he hunted the bee,
   The snake slipt under a spray,
The hawk stood with the down on his beak
   And stared, with his foot on the prey
And the nightingale thought, "I have sung many songs,
   But never a one so gay,
For he sings of what the world will be
   When the years have died away."

A Minuet of Mozart's
by Sara Teasdale

Across the dimly lighted room
   The violin drew wefts of sound,
   Airily they wove and wound
And glimmered gold against the gloom.

I watched the music turn to light,
   But at the pausing of the bow,
   The web was broken and the glow
Was drowned within the wave of night.

Lesson 11

Singers were an important part of temple service in Old Testament times.

Read Nehemiah 12:27–47. This passage describes the choir's part in dedicating the wall of Jerusalem.

Lesson 12

Have a Parent Share moment to share a story from your life or tell about a person who exemplifies this habit. Read and discuss the poem below.

"And the night shall be filled with music,
And the cares, that infest the day,
Shall fold their tents, like the Arabs,
And as silently steal away." — Henry Wadsworth Longfellow

Finish up with any other discussion, ideas, or celebration your family enjoys. Keep up this habit while going forth to concentrate on a new one.

Outdoor Life

Regularly enjoying and studying God's creation outdoors

Parent Prep

Read detailed thoughts about Outdoor Life on pages 135–137 of *Laying Down the Rails* and skim the lessons below.

♦ Goals for this Habit (and steps to get there)

_____

_____

_____

♦ A Person or Story from My Life that Demonstrates this Habit

_____

_____

_____

♦ Additional Stories, Poems, Quotations, Bible Verses I Want to Use

_____

_____

_____

_____

♦ Other Activities We Could Do to Practice this Habit

_____

_____

_____

♦ Celebration Ideas

_____

_____

_____

Most of the lessons for this habit contain descriptive poetry about nature. You may find it pleasant to enjoy these lessons outdoors.

Lesson 1

Read the definition and discuss Outdoor Life. Share with the children any goals you've identified for this habit (for instance, "We will spend one afternoon a week outdoors enjoying nature."). Also get their input on changes they think need to be made.

Read the Biblical principle found in Psalm 19:1–6 from your preferred version of the Bible. The psalms are full of nature references giving a general principle of enjoying the creation of God and seeing in it the glory of God.

Lesson 2

Discuss point one together, then read and discuss the two poems that follow.

 1. Regular time outdoors can affect your attitude and your health.

Snowballing
from *The Infant's Delight*

See these merry ones at play,
On this snowy New Year's Day:
How they run, and jump, and throw
Handfuls of the soft, white snow.
You should hear them laugh and shout
As they fling the snow about!
'Tis by Frank and Gus alone
That the balls are chiefly thrown,
While their cousins make and bring
Other balls for them to fling.
Katie is preparing thus,
Quite a store of balls for Gus;
But her merry sister May
From her task has run away,
All that heavy lump of snow,
At her cousin Gus to throw.
Edith is not very bold,
And at first she feared the cold;
Now at last you see her run
Down the steps to join the fun.

The Tables Turned
by William Wordsworth

Up! up! my Friend, and quit your books;
Or surely you'll grow double:
Up! up! my Friend, and clear your looks;
Why all this toil and trouble?

The sun above the mountain's head,
A freshening lustre mellow
Through all the long green fields has spread,
His first sweet evening yellow.

Books! 'tis a dull and endless strife:
Come, hear the woodland linnet,
How sweet his music! on my life,
There's more of wisdom in it.

Habit points from
Laying Down the Rails

And hark! how blithe the throstle sings!
He, too, is no mean preacher:
Come forth into the light of things,
Let Nature be your teacher.

She has a world of ready wealth,
Our minds and hearts to bless—
Spontaneous wisdom breathed by health,
Truth breathed by cheerfulness.

One impulse from a vernal wood
May teach you more of man,
Of moral evil and of good,
Than all the sages can.

Sweet is the lore which Nature brings;
Our meddling intellect
Mis-shapes the beauteous forms of things:—
We murder to dissect.

Enough of Science and of Art;
Close up those barren leaves;
Come forth, and bring with you a heart
That watches and receives.

Lesson 3

Talk about point two. Read and discuss the quotation and the poem below. Make sure
your children know who George Washington Carver was. They will appreciate his words
more if they know the context of his life.

*"I love to think of nature as an unlimited broadcasting station, through which God
speaks to us every hour, if we will only tune in." — George Washington Carver*

 2. Nature study can be a source of delight no matter your age.

A Little Girl's Fancies
from *Harper's Third Reader*, edited by James Baldwin

O little flowers, you love me so,
   You could not do without me;
O little birds that come and go,
   You sing sweet songs about me;
O little moss, observed by few,
   That round the tree is creeping,
You like my head to rest on you
   When I am idly sleeping.

O rushes by the riverside,
   You bow when I come near you;

O fish, you leap about with pride,
    Because you think I hear you;
O river, you shine clear and bright,
    To tempt me to look in you;
O water lilies, pure and white,
    You hope that I shall win you.

O pretty things, you love me so,
    I see I must not leave you;
You find it very dull I know—
    I should dislike to grieve you.
Don't wrinkle up, you silly moss;
    My flowers, you need not shiver;
My little buds, don't look so cross;
    Don't talk so loud, my river!

I'm *telling* you I will not go—
    It's foolish to feel slighted;
It's rude to interrupt me so—
    You ought to be delighted.
Ah! now you're growing good, I see,
    Though anger is beguiling;
The pretty blossoms not at me—
    I see a robin smiling.

And I will make a promise, dears,
    That will content you, maybe:
I'll love you through the happy years,
    Till I'm a nice old lady!
True love, like yours and mine, they say,
    Can never think of ceasing,
But year by year, and day by day,
    Keeps steadily increasing.

Lesson 4

Discuss point three, sharing pointers on how to marvel over and care for creation. Then read and discuss the poem, "Maker of Heaven and Earth."

 3. Not everyone needs to be an expert, but each person should marvel over and care for God's creation.

Activity: Plan any kind of outdoor activity where you will be around nature. Go to a zoo, take a hike, fish at a pond, roller skate or bike ride, have a picnic, canoe or paddle boat, play in an empty field, climb a tree. Keep plenty of water around and a cheerful attitude. Being outdoors can be done even in cold weather. It has been said that there is no bad weather, just bad bundling.

Maker of Heaven and Earth
by Cecil Frances Alexander

All things bright and beautiful,
   All creatures great and small,
All things wise and wonderful,
   The Lord God made them all.

Each little flower that opens,
   Each little bird that sings,
He made their glowing colours,
   He made their tiny wings.

The rich man in his castle,
   The poor man at his gate,
God made them, high or lowly,
   And ordered their estate.

The purple-headed mountain,
   The river running by,
The sunset, and the morning,
   That brightens up the sky;

The cold wind in the winter,
   The pleasant summer sun,
The ripe fruits in the garden,
   He made them every one.

The tall trees in the greenwood,
   The meadows where we play,
The rushes by the water,
   We gather every day;—

He gave us eyes to see them,
   And lips that we might tell,
How great is God Almighty,
   Who has made all things well.

Feed minds. Inspire hearts. Encourage action.

Lesson 5

Read and discuss the quotation and the poem below.

   "To me a lush carpet of pine needles or spongy grass is more welcome than the most luxurious Persian rug." — Helen Keller

Read Genesis 2:4–17. When God made man and then made a home for him, that home was a beautiful garden. Not only was it man's home, but he had productive work to do in the garden.

The Use of Flowers
by Mary Howitt

God might have bade the earth bring forth
   Enough for great and small,
The oak tree, and the cedar tree,
   Without a flower at all.

He might have made enough, enough,
   For every want of ours;
For luxury, medicine, and toil,
   And yet have had no flowers.

The ore within the mountain mine
   Requireth none to grow,
Nor doth it need the lotus flower
   To make the river flow.

The clouds might give abundant rain,
   The nightly dews might fall,
And the herb that keepeth life in man
   Might yet have drank them all.

Then wherefore, wherefore were they made
   All dyed with rainbow light,
All fashioned with supremest grace,
   Upspringing day and night:—

Springing in valleys green and low,
   And on the mountains high,
And in the silent wilderness
   Where no man passeth by?

Our outward life requires them not,—
   Then wherefore had they birth?—
To minister delight to man,
   To beautify the earth;

To comfort man,—to whisper hope,
   Whene'er his faith is dim,
For who so careth for the flowers
   Will much more care for him!

Lesson 6

Read and discuss the quotation and poem that follows.

"Look deep into nature, and then you will understand everything better." — *Albert Einstein*

The School
from *Harper's Third Reader*, edited by James Baldwin

"Little girl, where do you go to school,
    And when do you go, little girl?
Over the grass from dawn till dark,
    Your feet are in a whirl;
Like the wind you ramble everywhere,
    And like the birds you sing;
But what have you learned in your books at school?
Do you know all the tables? Can you write every rule?"

Then the little girl answered—
    Only stopping to cling
To my finger a minute,
    As the bird on the wing
Catches a twig of willow
    And stops to twitter and sing—

"When the daisies' eyes are a-twinkle
    With happy tears of dew;
When swallows waken in the eaves,
    And the lamb bleats to the ewe;
When the lawns are striped with golden bars,
    And the light of the sun puts out the stars;
When morning's breath is fresh and cool,
It is then that I haste on my way to school.

"My school roof is the deep blue sky;
    And the bells that ring for me there
Are all the voices of morning
    Afloat in the dewy air.
Kind Nature is my teacher;
    And the book from which I spell
Is thumb-worn by the hills and brooks,
    Where I learn my lessons well."

Thus the little girl answered,
    In her happy outdoor tone.
She was up to my pocket,
    I was a man full grown;
But the next time that she goes to school,
    She will not go alone.

Lesson 7

Have a Parent Share moment to share a story from your life or tell about a person who exemplifies Outdoor Life, then read and discuss the poem below.

"To one who has been long in city pent,
    'Tis very sweet to look into the fair
And open face of heaven,—to breathe a prayer

Full in the smile of the blue firmament." — John Keats

Lesson 8

Read and discuss the quotation below. Make sure the children know who Lindbergh was and his accomplishment.

"In the wilderness I sense the miracle of life, and behind it our scientific accomplishments fade to trivia." — *Charles A. Lindbergh*

Read Psalm 104. This psalm provides great substance for thought of God when you are out in nature.

Lesson 9

Read and discuss the quotation below.

"Great things are done when men and mountains meet. This is not done by jostling in the street." — *William Blake*

Activity: Take some time outdoors to really study an object of nature in its natural setting. Observe it closely. Let the children point out what they see. Ask them questions to get them to see more. Field guides can be helpful for identification, but don't worry too much if you can't find the name for the object you observe. You could sketch the object. After a little time of observation, let the children run around and have fun outside.

Lesson 10

Read and discuss the quotation and poems below.

"To sit in the shade on a fine day and look upon verdure is the most perfect refreshment." — *Jane Austen*

Verdure is lush green vegetation.

Trees
by Joyce Kilmer

I think that I shall never see
A poem as lovely as a tree.

A tree whose hungry mouth is pressed
Against the sweet earth's flowing breast;

A tree that looks at God all day,
And lifts her leafy arms to pray;

A tree that may in summer wear
A nest of robins in her hair;

Upon whose bosom snow has lain;
Who intimately lives with rain.

Poems are made by fools like me,
But only God can make a tree.

Remember that you can use quotations or poems for copywork or recitation lessons.

Stars
by Sara Teasdale

Alone in the night
  On a dark hill
With pines around me
  Spicy and still,

And a heaven full of stars
  Over my head,
White and topaz
  And misty red;

Myriads with beating
  Hearts of fire
That aeons
  Cannot vex or tire;

Up the dome of heaven
  Like a great hill,
I watch them marching
  Stately and still,

And I know that I
  Am honored to be
Witness
  Of so much majesty.

Lesson 11

Read and discuss the quotation and the poem that follows. Be sure the children know who Galileo was and his relationship to what he said about "the sun, with all those planets revolving around it."

"The sun, with all those planets revolving around it and dependent on it, can still ripen a bunch of grapes as if it had nothing else in the universe to do." — *Galileo*

The Sunshine
by Mary Howitt

I love the sunshine everywhere,—
  In wood, and field, and glen;
I love it in the busy haunts
  Of town-imprisoned men.

I love it when it streameth in
  The humble cottage door
And casts the chequered casement shade
  Upon the red-brick floor.

I love it where the children lie
   Deep in the clovery grass,
To watch among the twining roots
   The gold-green beetles pass.

I love it on the breezy sea,
   To glance on sail and oar,
While the great waves, like molten glass,
   Come leaping to the shore.

I love it on the mountain-tops,
   Where lies the thawless snow,
And half a kingdom, bathed in light,
   Lies stretching out below.

And when it shines in forest-glades,
   Hidden, and green, and cool,
Through mossy boughs and veined leaves,
   How is it beautiful!

How beautiful on little stream,
   When sun and shade at play,
Make silvery meshes, while the brook
   Goes singing on its way.

How beautiful, where dragon-flies
   Are wondrous to behold,
With rainbow wings of gauzy pearl,
   And bodies blue and gold!

How beautiful, on harvest-slopes,
   To see the sunshine lie!
Or on the paler reaped fields,
   Where yellow shocks stand high!

Oh, yes! I love the sunshine!
   Like kindness or like mirth
Upon a human countenance,
   Is sunshine on the earth—

Upon the earth; upon the sea;
   And through the crystal air,
Or piled up cloud; the gracious sun
   Is glorious everywhere!

Lesson 12

Finish up with any other discussion, ideas, or celebration your family enjoys. Keep up this habit while going forth to concentrate on a new one.

Quick Perception of Senses

Being aware of things around you
that you can see, hear, feel, taste, or smell

Parent Prep

Read detailed thoughts about Quick Perception of Senses on pages 137–139 of *Laying Down the Rails* and skim the lessons below.

♦ Goals for this Habit (and steps to get there)

_____

_____

_____

♦ A Person or Story from My Life that Demonstrates this Habit

_____

_____

_____

♦ Additional Stories, Poems, Quotations, Bible Verses I Want to Use

_____

_____

_____

♦ Other Activities We Could Do to Practice this Habit

_____

_____

_____

♦ Celebration Ideas

_____

_____

_____

Plan for lots of activities and games throughout this training to help develop Quick Perception of Senses. Several activities are suggested in points 3, 4, and 6 in the sidebar.

Lesson 1

Read the definition and discuss Quick Perception of Senses. Share with the children any goals you've identified for this habit (for instance, "We will plan regular games that help develop a quick perception of senses."). Also get their input on changes they think need to be made.

Read the Biblical principle found in 1 Samuel 3:2–10 from your preferred version of the

Bible. Samuel did not ignore the calls of God. He responded to God's voice.

Lesson 2

Discuss point one, then read and discuss "The Bootblack from Ann Street."

 1. **Use all your senses and observe all that you can about objects around you: shades of color: relative temperature; degrees of hardness, texture, and size.**

Charlotte Mason called the exercise described in point one "Sensory Gymnastics."

The Bootblack from Ann Street
from *An American Book of Golden Deeds* by James Baldwin

Several years ago near the corner of Park Row and Beekman Street, New York, there stood a large frame building. It was four or five stories in height. On the ground floor there were several stores; the upper floors were occupied by offices.

Like all the old-fashioned buildings of that time, it contained but one stairway, and there was no fire escape. Elevators had not yet come into use. The only way, therefore, of passing to or from the upper rooms was by means of the rickety wooden stairs. No such building would now be permitted to exist in the city.

One cold day in January the end came to that old structure. A fire broke out, nobody knew exactly where. The stairway was soon filled with smoke and flame. The people in the offices above were cut off—there seemed to be no way for them to escape. Some were burned to death. Some were smothered by the smoke. A few were rescued from the windows by means of ladders.

Parental Discretion Advisory: A couple of the sentences in this story may be too intense for sensitive children. Edit as needed.

The Fire Department was not then equipped as it is now. There were no ladders long enough to reach to the topmost floor; and yet there were three men on that floor looking out at a window and calling for help. What could be done to save them? Was there no way of getting them down from their perilous position? If they remained where they were, the flames would soon reach and destroy them. If they leaped to the pavement below, they would surely be crushed to death.

While the firemen were vainly throwing water on the flames, and everybody was wondering what should be done, a little bootblack rushed into the crowd. He saw the men, with hopeless, beseeching faces, standing at the window. He saw, too, what no other person had seen, the only way of saving them.

"Hey there! give me that jimmy!" he cried, and he snatched a wrench from the hands of a mechanic who was standing by. He rushed to a telegraph pole that stood directly across the street from the burning building. In a moment he was "shinning it" up the pole, with the heavy wrench stuck in his belt.

"What's he going to do up there?" inquired the bystanders. Then they noticed for the first time that a wire rope—a stay rope, as it was called—extended from the top of the pole to the roof of the building at a point just above the window where the men were standing. If the rope could be cut from the pole, it would fall right across the window, and the men could slide down it to the ground.

Not a moment was to be lost. The fire was already beginning to take hold of the woodwork beneath the window. The smoke was rolling up in heavy clouds. The wind was blowing a gale. Would the little fellow ever get to the top of the pole? Small though he was, he was agile and strong, and he went up rapidly. When he reached the first crosspiece, the crowd below him gave a great cheer. In another moment he was on the upper crosspiece, his wrench was in his hands, he was hard at work twisting the wire rope from its fastening. The crowd cheered again.

Oh, how well that rope was fastened, and how long it took to loosen it! But at last it fell. It fell just as the boy expected it to fall, and hung straight down in front of the window. The men saw it. They seized it, and one after another slid quickly down to the ground. A few minutes later the whole of the upper floor of the building fell in with a fearful crash.

The little hero who had saved three lives by his quick wit came leisurely down the telegraph pole, returned the wrench to its owner, and again mingled with the crowd. He did not expect to be rewarded. He never thought of thanks. He had only done his duty.

"Where is the boy who cut that wire?" inquired a gentleman who had seen the brave deed.

"Yes, where is he?" inquired others, seeming now to remember that he deserved some reward. "Who is he?"

"Oh, it's Charlie Wright, the little bootblack from Ann Street," said one who knew him.

An agent of the American Humane Society soon afterward found him busy at work in his accustomed place. "Well, Charlie," he said, "you did a brave and noble deed, and our society wishes to thank you for it by giving you a medal."

The story of his exploit was told in London. The English Humane Society wished also to thank him, and it sent him a gold medal inscribed with these words:

PRESENTED TO CHARLES WRIGHT, FOR SAVING THREE LIVES.

Lesson 3

Talk over point two and the Shakespeare quotation that follows.

 2. **Daily sensory gymnastics are not the same as nature study but can supplement and support nature study.**

"How use doth breed a habit in a man!" — *William Shakespeare*

Lesson 4

Discuss point five.

 5. **The best way to cultivate the senses is by getting to know the world of nature.**

Activity: Play the sensory game described by Charlotte in point three in the sidebar. Tell each child they will discover what an object is by using only one of their senses. Pass around an object (such as bread) and let the children first use their sense of smell. Then a different object can be discovered using only touch; you could put the object in a bag and allow each child to reach in and feel the object but not look at it. Alternately, you could challenge the child to draw the object hidden in the bag, using only his sense of touch to try to visualize it in his mind and on paper.

Lesson 5

Read Exodus 3:1–6. Moses observed a bush on fire but noticed that it did not burn up.

3. Occasionally give your child an object and ask him to tell all that he can discover about it by using only one of his senses; for example, touch.

4. Play a game of "What Can You Remember?" to cultivate this habit.

Notes

 6. Encourage your child to observe his surroundings by randomly asking whether he noticed accurately a particular thing that you noticed.

Talk about point seven. Quick Observation of the Senses is important in situations such as crossing a street, driving a car, taking care of babies, etc. The more you train your senses to perceive quickly now, the better you will be at those responsibilities when they come your way.

7. Young children are naturally observant, but developing the habit of observation will help you continue the skill even as you grow older.

Lesson 6

Read and discuss "The Crow and the Pitcher." Perceiving available resources coupled with quick wit results in creative solutions.

The Crow and the Pitcher
from *The Aesop for Children* by Milo Winter

In a spell of dry weather, when the Birds could find very little to drink, a thirsty Crow found a pitcher with a little water in it. But the pitcher was high and had a narrow neck, and no matter how he tried, the Crow could not reach the water. The poor thing felt as if he must die of thirst.

Then an idea came to him. Picking up some small pebbles, he dropped them into the pitcher one by one. With each pebble the water rose a little higher until at last it was near enough so he could drink.

In a pinch, a good use of our wits may help us out.

Lesson 7

Help children find the memory device that works best for them for the activity below. It could be taking a mental picture or linking one object to another in some way or singing the names of objects to themselves.

Activity: Have a game of "What Can You Remember?" as described by Charlotte (point four in the sidebar) or go to a busy place (the mall, a park, a walk down the street) and have the children stop and remember a scene that was just passed or bit of conversation heard.

The game "What Can You Remember?" simply involves a number of objects (Charlotte mentioned 100.) set on a table where the children can observe them for three minutes or so. You would then have the children leave the room to write down the names of as many objects as they can remember. Younger children can whisper the objects to you as you write down what they remember.

Lesson 8

Pay attention to animals' cues. They often can see, smell, hear, or sense better than we humans can.

Read Numbers 22:21–35. Balaam was not quick in sensing what his donkey sensed. The donkey was quick and responsive, however, and saved Balaam's life.

Lesson 9

Have a Parent Share moment to share a story from your life or tell about a person who exemplifies Quick Perception of Senses.

Lesson 10

Continue doing sensory gymnastics for as long as you need the practice to establish this habit. Then finish up with any other discussion, ideas, or celebration your family enjoys. Keep up this habit while going forth to concentrate on a new one.

Self-Control in Emergencies
*Thinking clearly and keeping emotions in check
no matter the circumstances*

Parent Prep

Read detailed thoughts about Self-Control in Emergencies on pages 139–141 of *Laying Down the Rails* and skim the lessons below.

♦ Goals for this Habit (and steps to get there)

_____

_____

_____

♦ A Person or Story from My Life that Demonstrates this Habit

_____

_____

_____

♦ Additional Stories, Poems, Quotations, Bible Verses I Want to Use

_____

_____

_____

♦ Other Activities We Could Do to Practice this Habit

_____

_____

_____

♦ Celebration Ideas

_____

_____

_____

Lesson 1

Read the definition and discuss Self-Control in Emergencies. Share with the children any goals you've identified for this habit (for instance, "We will practice breathing techniques that help one calm down when under stress."). Also get their input on changes they think need to be made.

Read the Biblical principle found in 1 Peter 5:8 from your preferred version of the Bible.

We must be self-controlled and alert to fight spiritual battles; the principle applies to our earthly struggles also.

Lesson 2

Discuss point one together, describing such a person to give a picture of what is expected. Then read and discuss "A Quick-Witted Mountain Girl."

 1. A person who can keep presence of mind can be of great service to others.

Lesson time is not the embodiment of habit training. It gives the family inspiration and thoughts to ponder as you practice your habit throughout the day.

A Quick-Witted Mountain Girl
from *An American Book of Golden Deeds* by James Baldwin

On a hillside overlooking a deep ravine in Colorado stood the little brown house which Nora O'Neill called her home. There was very little level ground near it. The front yard sloped downward, five hundred feet or more, to a broad ledge of solid rock at the foot of which was a railroad track. On the farther side of the track the land again dipped steeply down to the bottom of the ravine, where ran a roaring mountain stream. At the back of the house the hill rose mountain high and was covered with a dense growth of stunted trees and straggling underwoods.

One evening as Nora was helping her mother with the kitchen work they heard a rumbling, rattling sound on the railroad track below them.

"What is that, mother?" asked Nora, running to the door to listen.

"Oh, it's nothing but the handcar going back to town with the men," answered her mother, whose hearing was by no means the sharpest.

"Well, I never heard it make that kind of noise," said Nora. "It sounded more like a coal wagon unloading coal, and not at all like the handcar. I have a notion to go down and see what it was."

"Nonsense, Nora," said her mother. "You're only wanting to shirk your work. Look at the clock. It's just about the time the men always go back. They'll barely get to the station and lift the car off the track before the Rio Grande express goes by."

Nora said no more. She finished her work and then went to the door to listen for the coming express. Soon she heard a faint whistle echoing down the valley through the dusky twilight. The train was skirting the farther side of the great bend and, by way of the winding road, was still several miles distant. Nora ran down to the side of the track to wait for its coming. She had done this every evening through the summer and it was a source of much enjoyment to her. She liked to see the great coaches glide past, each one brilliant with light and full of well-dressed travelers.

"I wonder where all those people come from and where they are going," she often said to herself.

She was scarcely halfway down to the track when she was surprised to see something like a dark shadow lying across it. What could it be?

She hastened her footsteps. Soon it was all plain to her. A big boulder with several smaller rocks had become loosened from its place above and had slid down upon the rails. No doubt it had fallen soon after the handcar had passed down, and it was this which she and her mother had heard.

What should she do? The express would be there within less than five minutes. There was no time for thought.

She pushed against the boulder with all her strength. She might as well have pushed

Habit points from *Laying Down the Rails*

against the mountain itself, and this she knew in a moment.

Then she turned and ran back toward the house faster than you or I could run up so steep a hill.

"Quick, mother, quick!" she cried. "The oil can! the oil can!"

As she ran she picked up a stick of dry pine that was lying by the path. The can of kerosene was in its usual place. She seized it and dashed the oil over one end of the stick. She had seen her father do this once when he was in haste for a light. It was his way of making a torch.

"Are you crazy, child?" cried her mother.

But Nora did not hear. She quickly lighted the stick in the fire of the kitchen stove. Then, holding her blazing torch high above her head, she ran down the hill by another path in the direction of the train.

The roar of the great express could now be plainly heard. Nora reached the track not a moment too soon.

"What in the world does that mean?" said the engineer as, peering through the dusk, he saw a girl with a flaming torch standing on the road. He did not know that, just around the next short curve, destruction was lurking. He blew the whistle; the girl did not stir. He threw on the brakes as hard as they would go. The train slowed up suddenly, but not too soon.

Nora leaped aside as the pitiless engine rolled past her. It rolled on around the curve. It came to a standstill just as its pilot struck the great boulder.

"What is the matter?" cried the passengers, rushing out in great alarm.

"Matter enough," said the engineer. "Do you see that boulder on the tracks? If this girl had not signaled us just in time, the whole train would have gone down into the gully there. We all owe our lives to her."

The passengers crowded around Nora. The women kissed her. The men thanked her a dozen times over. She told her story in answer to their questions. A purse full of silver and greenbacks was offered to her.

"I didn't do it for pay," she said. "And besides, it wasn't much to do. It wasn't worth so much money."

"You have saved perhaps a dozen lives," said the conductor, "and certainly that is a good deal to do. We shall never be able to pay you all that we owe you."

Help soon arrived. The boulder was removed and the track was repaired. Then the train moved away while more than one of the passengers called down heaven's blessing upon the child whose golden deed had saved their lives that night.

Lesson 3

Talk over point two.

 2. Keep a calm spirit no matter what happens around you.

Activity: Practice different breathing techniques that calm one down when hyperventilation wants to set in.

- ♦ One technique is a normal breath. Place a hand on your stomach and a hand on your chest. Take in a normal amount of air through your nose. As you inhale, the hand on your stomach should rise, while the hand on your chest should stay still. Exhale normally and repeat.
- ♦ A calming technique is to take a deep breath in through your nose and hold it for a few seconds. Exhale through your lips and relax your eyes, your face, and the rest of your body.

Lesson 4

Discuss point three, then read and discuss the story, "Partners."

 3. Remember that physical calmness can promote mental calmness, just as mental calmness can result in physical calmness.

Partners
from *An American Book of Golden Deeds* by James Baldwin

Little Mackie, as his friends called him, was an inmate of the Hospital for Crippled Children. He was a small boy and his years were few, yet his face was already drawn and seamed with lines of suffering. One of his feet was twisted and the other almost useless; yet he could hobble around very nimbly on his crutches, and he took great pleasure in helping other boys who were worse off than himself.

His particular friend and crony was Dannie O'Connell, whose cot adjoined his own. Dannie was a helpless little fellow, with legs that were no better than none and a back so weak that he could not sit up without props. Many were the hours which little Mackie spent at Dannie's bedside, and many were the words of encouragement and hope that he poured into the ears of the helpless child.

"We're partners, Dannie," he would say. "When I get bigger I'll be a bootblack down on the Square, and you and me'll go halvers in the profits."

"But what could I do?" queried Dannie. "I couldn't help with the business. Why, I can't even hold myself up."

"Oh, you'll be lots better by that time," answered the ever hopeful Mackie. "I'll get you a high chair with wheels under it, so that I can trundle you around. And I'll get a little candy stand at the corner for you to 'tend to. I'll shine 'em up for the fine gentlemen that come that way, and you'll sell candy to the ladies. They'll all want to trade with you when they see you sitting there in your high chair."

"I think it will be very nice," sighed Dannie; and he lay gazing up toward the ceiling and trying to forget his troubles.

"Of course it will be nice," said Mackie; "and don't you forget that we'll be partners."

One night when all the children were in their cots an alarm was sounded. What could it mean? Soon the cry of fire was heard, and then a great rushing and hurrying in the halls and on the stairways. Little Mackie jumped up and seized his crutches, and all the other boys in the ward began to cry out in alarm. But their nurse soothed them and told them that they need not be afraid, for she was quite sure that the fire was in a distant part of the building, and would soon be put out.

Little Mackie lay down again, but he kept his eyes wide open. "Hey, Dannie, partner," he whispered, very softly, "don't be scared. I'm watching out for you, and nurse says there's no danger."

The noise outside grew louder, and there was more of it. Mackie could hear the people running. He could hear the children screaming in the other wards. Soon he saw the red light of the flames shining through the narrow window above the door. Then he smelled the smoke and saw it coming into the room through every crevice and crack. The nurse turned pale with fear and did not seem to know what to do.

Then three men rushed in—firemen with big hats on their heads and waterproof capes on their shoulders. Each took two children in his arms and with the fainting nurse hurried away through the strangling smoke.

Remember that some lessons might better suit older or younger children. Use those that best fit your family situation.

"Be brave! We'll be back for you in a minute," said one of them as he ran past Dannie and Mackie.

The two "partners" were left alone in the room. Mackie could hear the crackling and roaring of the flames. He could even see them creeping along the floor and licking up the carpet in the lower hallway. He could feel their hot breath. In another minute they would reach the wooden stairs, and then how could any one ever come up to save the children that were still in the wards?

"Run, Mackie!" cried Dannie, trying in vain to sit up. "I guess they forgot to come back. Run, Mackie, and don't wait for me."

"No, I don't run, so long as you're my partner," said Mackie.

He was leaning on his crutches by the side of Dannie's cot.

"Put your arms round my neck, Dannie. That's how. Now hold on, tight! Snuggle your face down over my shoulder. That's right; now we'll go. Hold fast, and don't swallow any more smoke than you can help, Dannie."

Clack! clack! clack! Through the smothering smoke the little crutches clattered out of the room and into the burning hallway. And Dannie, with his arms clasped around his partner's neck, and his shriveled legs dangling helplessly behind, was borne half-fainting through the fearful din.

Clack! clack! clack! Mackie was so short and his head was so near to the floor that he escaped the thickest part of the smoke, which rolled in clouds toward the ceiling. He hurried to the stairway, keeping his face bent downward and his eyes half closed. He did not dare to speak to Dannie, for he had no breath to spare.

Outside of the building there were many busy hands and many anxious faces.

"Have all the children been saved?" asked one of the managers of the hospital.

"Oh, sir, not all," was the sad answer. "There were a few in the upper wards who could not be saved, the fire spread so rapidly. And there are still two little boys in the lower ward whom it is impossible to reach."

"Surely these boys ought to be rescued," cried the manager. "Won't some one try to reach them?"

"Sir," answered a helper who had already carried ten children out of the flaming building, "it is too late. The stairways are all blazing and the ward itself is full of fire."

In fact, the flames could now be seen bursting out of every window.

Clack! clack! clack!

What sound was that on the marble steps before the smoke-filled door of the doomed hospital? It was not a loud noise, but those who stood nearest heard it quite plainly amid all the other sounds, the snapping of the burning wood, the roaring of the flames, the falling of heavy timbers.

Then right out from beneath the cloud of smoke came little Mackie, bearing Dannie upon his shoulders. Helping hands were stretched forth to receive him, and the brave lad fell fainting in the arms of a big policeman.

Dannie was scarcely harmed at all, though dreadfully frightened. But Mackie's poor hands were badly scorched and his eyebrows were singed off. His nightshirt was burned through in a dozen places. His bare, crippled feet were blistered by the fallen coals he had stepped upon. His little body was full of hurts and burns. Kind arms carried him to a place of safety; but for a long time he lay senseless to all that was happening around him.

When at last he awoke to consciousness his first thought was to inquire for Dannie. Then, as he turned painfully in the little bed where they had laid him, he closed his eyes again and said, "Me and Dannie are partners, don't you know?"

Lesson 5

Read and discuss the quotation.

"Nothing gives one person so much advantage over another as to remain always cool and unruffled under all circumstances." — *Thomas Jefferson*

Read Genesis 25:29–34. Esau was so hungry and exhausted that he thought he was dying and did not display self-control. Instead he sold his birthright to his crafty brother for a bowl of soup.

Lesson 6

Being prepared helps one to stay calm in emergencies.

Activity: Take the time to train (or provide training for) your children for different emergencies. Depending on their ages, you could teach them

- how to dial 911 and state their emergency.
- fire drills.
- what to do if a stranger approaches them.
- first aid.
- what to do if someone is choking or not breathing.
- wilderness survival.
- what to do if they find themselves lost.
- address, phone number and parents' names.
- what to do if a dish breaks in the kitchen and shatters across the floor.

Lesson 7

A surety of spirit and strength of character allow one to lead in a crisis when others are afraid. Read and discuss the story of "The Dark Day" and the related poem that follows.

The Dark Day
from *Fifty Famous People* by James Baldwin

Listen, and I will tell you of the famous dark day in Connecticut. It was in the month of May, more than a hundred years ago.

The sun rose bright and fair, and the morning was without a cloud. The air was very still. There was not a breath of wind to stir the young leaves on the trees.

Then, about the middle of the day, it began to grow dark. The sun was hidden. A black cloud seemed to cover the earth.

The birds flew to their nests. The chickens went to roost. The cows came home from the pasture and stood mooing at the gate. It grew so dark that the people could not see their way along the streets.

Then everybody began to feel frightened. "What is the matter? What is going to happen?" each one asked of another. The children cried. The dogs howled. The women wept, and some of the men prayed.

"The end of the world has come!" cried some; and they ran about in the darkness.

"This is the last great day!" cried others; and they knelt down and waited.

In the old statehouse, the wise men of Connecticut were sitting. They were men who made the laws, and much depended upon their wisdom.

When the darkness came, they too began to be alarmed. The gloom was terrible.

"It is the day of the Lord," said one.

"No use to make laws," said another, "for they will never be needed."

"I move that we adjourn," said a third.

Then up from his seat rose Abraham Davenport. His voice was clear and strong, and all knew that he, at least, was not afraid.

"This may be the last great day," he said. "I do not know whether the end of the world has come or not. But I am sure that it is my duty to stand at my post as long as I live. So, let us go on with the work that is before us. Let the candles be lighted."

His words put courage into every heart. The candles were brought in. Then with his strong face aglow in their feeble light, he made a speech in favor of a law to help poor fishermen.

And as he spoke, the other lawmakers listened in silence till the darkness began to fade and the sky grew bright again.

The people of Connecticut still remember Abraham Davenport, because he was a wise judge and a brave lawmaker. The poet Whittier has written a poem about him, which you will like to hear.

Abraham Davenport
by John Greenleaf Whittier, adapted

'Twas on a May-day of the far old year
Seventeen hundred eighty, that there fell
Over the bloom and sweet life of the Spring,
Over the fresh earth and the heaven of noon,
A horror of great darkness, like the night
In day of which the Norland sagas tell,—
The Twilight of the Gods. The low-hung sky
Was black with ominous clouds, save where its rim
Was fringed with a dull glow, like that which climbs
The crater's sides from the red hell below.
Birds ceased to sing, and all the barnyard fowls
Roosted; the cattle at the pasture bars
Lowed, and looked homeward; bats on leathern wings
Flitted abroad; the sounds of labor died;
Men prayed, and women wept; all ears grew sharp
To hear the doom-blast of the trumpet shatter
The black sky, that the dreadful face of Christ
Might look from the rent clouds, not as He looked
A loving guest at Bethany, but stern
As Justice and inexorable Law.

Meanwhile in the old State House, dim as ghosts,
Sat the lawgivers of Connecticut,
Trembling beneath their legislative robes.
"It is the Lord's Great Day! Let us adjourn,"
Some said; and then, as if with one accord,
All eyes were turned to Abraham Davenport.
He rose, slow cleaving with his steady voice
The intolerable hush. "This well may be
The Day of Judgment which the world awaits;

But be it so or not, I only know
My present duty, and my Lord's command
To occupy till He come. So at the post
Where He hath set me in His providence,
I choose, for one, to meet Him face to face,—
No faithless servant frightened from my task,
But ready when the Lord of the harvest calls;
And therefore, with all reverence, I would say,
Let God do His work, we will see to ours.
Bring in the candles." And they brought them in.

Then by the flaring lights the Speaker read,
Albeit with husky voice and shaking hands,
An act to amend an act to regulate
The shad and alewive fisheries. Whereupon
Wisely and well spake Abraham Davenport,
Straight to the question, with no figures of speech
Save the ten Arab signs, yet not without
The shrewd dry humor natural to the man:
His awe-struck colleagues listening all the while,
Between the pauses of his argument,
To hear the thunder of the wrath of God
Break from the hollow trumpet of the cloud.

And there he stands in memory to this day,
Erect, self-poised, a rugged face, half seen
Against the background of unnatural dark,
A witness to the ages as they pass,
That simple duty hath no place for fear.

Lesson 8

Going to God in prayer is a great first step in emergencies. A quick prayer sent up can put you in the frame of mind that God is ultimately in control and will be with you as you decide your course of action.

Read Genesis 32:3–21 and 33:11. Jacob heard of his brother Esau's coming with 400 men and was afraid. Despite his fear, he acted shrewdly in sending gifts ahead and dividing up his family and possessions.

Lesson 9

Have a Parent Share moment to share a story from your life or tell about a person who exemplifies Self-Control in Emergencies, then discuss the quotation below. You might also think of service positions that require Self-Control in Emergencies, like firefighters or policemen. Cultivating this habit now can be a great asset if you serve in a capacity like that in the future.

"A hero is no braver than an ordinary man, but he is braver five minutes longer."
— *Ralph Waldo Emerson*

Lesson 10

Finish up with any other discussion, ideas, or celebration your family enjoys. Keep up this habit while going forth to concentrate on a new one.

Self-Discipline in Habits
Regulating oneself to continue doing the good habits learned

Parent Prep

Read detailed thoughts about Self-Discipline in Habits on pages 142 and 143 of *Laying Down the Rails* and skim the lessons below.

♦ Goals for this Habit (and steps to get there)

_____

_____

_____

♦ A Person or Story from My Life that Demonstrates this Habit

_____

_____

_____

♦ Additional Stories, Poems, Quotations, Bible Verses I Want to Use

_____

_____

_____

♦ Other Activities We Could Do to Practice this Habit

_____

_____

_____

♦ Celebration Ideas

_____

_____

_____

Self-control is not *doing something even when you feel like it; for example, not panicking in an emergency even though you want to. Self-discipline is doing something even when you* don't *feel like it; for example, getting out of bed in the morning even when you don't want to.*

Lesson 1

Read the definition and discuss Self-Discipline in Habits. Share with the children any goals you've identified for this habit (for instance, "We will find one habit that each family member needs extra practice in and concentrate our efforts in training our wills toward those habits."). Also get their input on changes they think need to be made.

Read the Biblical principle found in 1 Timothy 6:11 from your preferred version of the Bible. We are to chase after righteousness and godliness and endurance.

Lesson 2

Discuss point one. A parent's discipline is needed at first in order to help children advance to *self*-discipline. But then the child must take up the mantle for himself. Read and discuss "The Thief and His Mother."

 1. Training in good habits is not complete until you continue doing the habit by yourself.

The Thief and His Mother
adapted from *Aesop's Fables,* translated by George Fyler Townsend

A boy stole a lesson-book from one of his schoolfellows and took it home to his Mother. She not only abstained from beating him, but encouraged him. He next time stole a cloak and brought it to her, and she again commended him. The Youth, advanced to adulthood, proceeded to steal things of still greater value. At last he was caught in the very act, and having his hands bound behind him, was led away to the place of public execution. His Mother followed in the crowd and violently beat her breast in sorrow, whereupon the young man said, 'I wish to say something to my Mother in her ear.' She came close to him, and he roared violently in her ear. The Mother upbraided him as an unnatural child, whereon he replied, 'Ah! If you had beaten me when I first stole and brought to you that lesson-book, I should not have come to this, nor have been thus led to a disgraceful death.'

3. Make the transition from supervised habits to self-disciplined habits in small steps.

Lesson 3

Talk over point two together. Weekends, holidays, time at grandparents, grocery shopping—these are not times to relax discipline in habits. Read and discuss the quotation below.

 2. Consistency is a key to forming and continuing good habits—no matter the season or the location.

"A bad habit never disappears miraculously, it's an undo-it-yourself project." — Abigail Van Buren

Activity: Evaluate the habits your children have learned. You could have a discussion with each child and get his opinion about what habit he thinks he could use more work on. Take a week or two to concentrate on consistency in the training of that habit. Enlist the child's will: let your child see why he needs to train in this habit, inspire him with stories and living examples, pray with him and for him.

Lesson 4

Discuss point four.

 4. Aim toward good habits of action, body language, and words.

Read Luke 2:51 and 52 and 1 Samuel 2:26. The same description is given here of the boys Jesus and Samuel: growing in favor with God and man. They were young, but they chose to discipline themselves toward an obedient, humble life.

Habit points from *Laying Down the Rails*

Lesson 5

Good habits will help us give up selfish ways. A submissive life puts others before itself.

Prayer of St. Francis of Assisi
Lord, make me an instrument of your peace.
Where there is hatred, let me sow love;
    where there is injury, pardon;
    where there is doubt, faith;
    where there is despair, hope;
    where there is darkness, light;
    and where there is sadness, joy.

O Divine Master, grant that I may not so much seek
    to be consoled as to console;
    to be understood as to understand;
    to be loved as to love.
For it is in giving that we receive;
    it is in pardoning that we are pardoned;
    and it is in dying that we are born to eternal life. Amen.

Lesson 6

Read and discuss the quotation.

> *"He who postpones the hour of living rightly is like the rustic who waits for the river to run out before he crosses." — Horace*

Activity: For problem habits, let each child create (draw, write, computer design) a Goal Pledge. He can state the habit he wants to work on, along with the specific steps he will take to cement that habit and the reasons he wants to work on that habit. Let the children hang their Goal Pledges in a visible place in the home.

Lesson 7

Discuss how the following Scriptures relate to Self-Discipline in Habits.

    Proverbs 9:13–18—Folly is loud and undisciplined.
    1 Thessalonians 5:12–22—Avoid evil; hold on to good.
    1 Peter 2:11, 12—Live good lives among unbelievers.
    2 Peter 1:5–9—Continue adding to the good qualities you've developed.

Lesson 8

Have a Parent Share moment to share a story from your life or tell about a person who exemplifies Self-Discipline in Habits, then read and discuss the quotation.

> *"Some people regard discipline as a chore. For me, it is a kind of order that sets me free to fly." — Julie Andrews*

Lesson 9

Talk over the following quotations. You might have older children explain them to the younger ones.

> *"What you do when you don't have to, determines what you will be when you can no longer help it."* — *Rudyard Kipling*

> *"The more self-disciplined you are, the more you will progress."* — *Thomas a Kempis*

Lesson 10

Finish up with any other discussion, ideas, or celebration your family enjoys. Keep up this habit while going forth to concentrate on a new one.

Self-Restraint in Indulgences

Enjoying pleasure in moderation; not being controlled by desire

Parent Prep

Read detailed thoughts about Self-Restraint in Indulgences on pages 144 and 145 of *Laying Down the Rails* and skim the lessons below.

♦ Goals for this Habit (and steps to get there)

_____

_____

_____

♦ A Person or Story from My Life that Demonstrates this Habit

_____

_____

_____

♦ Additional Stories, Poems, Quotations, Bible Verses I Want to Use

_____

_____

_____

♦ Other Activities We Could Do to Practice this Habit

_____

_____

_____

♦ Celebration Ideas

_____

_____

_____

Charlotte wrote directly to young people about Indulgences and Self-Restraint in Volume 4, Book 1, pages 191–203.

Lesson 1

Read the definition and discuss Self-Restraint in Indulgences. Share with the children any goals you've identified for this habit (for instance, "We will find useful hobbies or interests on which to spend our free time."). Also get their input on changes they think need to be made.

Read the Biblical principle found in Proverbs 23:29–35 from your preferred version of the Bible. A good example is given of what happens when we indulge in too much wine. Think ahead of time about consequences instead of letting desire tempt you toward too much.

📖 *1. Provide for your child's basic needs and comforts in life so he won't be as apt to grasp at indulgences when opportunity presents itself.*

📖 *3. Be sure your child is getting enough rest. Be cautious about participating in so many activities that your child becomes fatigued.*

📖 Habit points from *Laying Down the Rails*

Lesson 2

Discuss point two.

 2. Be industrious in your free time.

Activity: Let the family compose a Top Ten list (or a Top Twenty list) of ways to use free time wisely.

Lesson 3

Talk about self-restraint in the areas of food and drink, sleep, and entertainment. Read and discuss "The Cup-bearer."

The Cup-bearer
from *Fifty Famous People* by James Baldwin

I

Long, long ago, there lived in Persia a little prince whose name was Cyrus.

He was not petted and spoiled like many other princes. Although his father was a king, Cyrus was brought up like the son of a common man.

He knew how to work with his hands. He ate only the plainest food. He slept on a hard bed. He learned to endure hunger and cold.

When Cyrus was twelve years old he went with his mother to Media to visit his grandfather. His grandfather, whose name was Astyages, was king of Media, and very rich and powerful.

Cyrus was so tall and strong and handsome that his grandfather was very proud of him. He wished the lad to stay with him in Media. He therefore gave him many beautiful gifts and everything that could please a prince.

One day King Astyages planned to make a great feast for the lad. The tables were to be laden with all kinds of food. There was to be music and dancing; and Cyrus was to invite as many guests as he chose.

The hour for the feast came. Everything was ready. The servants were there, dressed in fine uniforms. The musicians and dancers were in their places. But no guests came.

"How is this, my dear boy?" asked the king. "The feast is ready, but no one has come to partake of it."

"That is because I have not invited any one," said Cyrus. "In Persia we do not have such feasts. If any one is hungry, he eats some bread and meat, with perhaps a few cresses, and that is the end of it. We never go to all this trouble and expense of making a fine dinner in order that our friends may eat what is not good for them."

King Astyages did not know whether to be pleased or displeased.

"Well," said he, "all these rich foods that were prepared for the feast are yours. What will you do with them?"

"I think I will give them to our friends," said Cyrus.

So he gave one portion to the king's officer who had taught him to ride. Another portion he gave to an old servant who waited upon his grandfather. And the rest he divided among the young women who took care of his mother.

II

The king's cupbearer, Sarcas, was very much offended because he was not given a share of the feast. The king also wondered why this man, who was his favorite, should be so slighted.

"Why didn't you give something to Sarcas?" he asked.

"Well, truly," said Cyrus, "I do not like him. He is proud and overbearing. He thinks that he makes a fine figure when he waits on you."

"And so he does," said the king. "He is very skillful as a cupbearer."

"That may be so," answered Cyrus, "but if you will let me be your cupbearer tomorrow, I think I can serve you quite as well."

King Astyages smiled. He saw that Cyrus had a will of his own, and this pleased him very much.

"I shall be glad to see what you can do," he said. "Tomorrow, you shall be the king's cupbearer."

III

You would hardly have known the young prince when the time came for him to appear before his grandfather. He was dressed in the rich uniform of the cupbearer, and he came forward with much dignity and grace.

He carried a white napkin upon his arm, and held the cup of wine very daintily with three of his fingers. His manners were perfect. Sarcas himself could not have served the king half so well.

"Bravo! bravo!" cried his mother, her eyes sparkling with pride.

"You have done well" said his grandfather. "But you neglected one important thing. It is the rule and custom of the cupbearer to pour out a little of the wine and taste it before handing the cup to me. This you forgot to do."

"Indeed, grandfather, I did not forget it," answered Cyrus.

"Then why didn't you do it?" asked his mother.

"Because I believed there was poison in the wine."

"Poison, my boy!" cried King Astyages, much alarmed. "Poison! poison!"

"Yes, grandfather, poison. For the other day, when you sat at dinner with your officers, I noticed that the wine made you act queerly. After the guests had drunk quite a little of it, they began to talk foolishly and sing loudly; and some of them went to sleep. And you, grandfather, were as bad as the rest. You forgot that you were king. You forgot all your good manners. You tried to dance and fell upon the floor. I am afraid to drink anything that makes men act in that way."

"Didn't you ever see your father behave so?" asked the king.

"No, never," said Cyrus. "He does not drink merely to be drinking. He drinks to quench his thirst, and that is all."

When Cyrus became a man, he succeeded his father as king of Persia; he also succeeded his grandfather Astyages as king of Media. He was a very wise and powerful ruler, and he made his country the greatest of any that was then known. In history he is commonly called Cyrus the Great.

Lesson 4

Talk about how these Scriptures relate to Self-Restraint in Indulgences.

Proverbs 6:9–11—Too much sleep brings poverty.

Ecclesiastes 2:1–11—Too many possessions and too much entertainment is chasing after the wind.

Ecclesiastes 5:10–20—Love of money and excessive work to gain that money is meaningless.

Lesson 5

Sometimes people find importance in being in the spotlight, owning lots of fine things, or gaining prestige in their profession. They chase after these things, losing sleep, community, tranquility, and sometimes even leaving their spiritual lives behind. Finding a balance is key. Read and discuss the Aesop fable below.

The Town Mouse and the Country Mouse
from *The Aesop for Children* by Milo Winter

A Town Mouse once visited a relative who lived in the country. For lunch the Country Mouse served wheat stalks, roots, and acorns, with a dash of cold water for drink. The Town Mouse ate very sparingly, nibbling a little of this and a little of that, and by her manner making it very plain that she ate the simple food only to be polite.

After the meal the friends had a long talk, or rather the Town Mouse talked about her life in the city while the Country Mouse listened. They then went to bed in a cozy nest in the hedgerow and slept in quiet and comfort until morning. In her sleep the Country Mouse dreamed she was a Town Mouse with all the luxuries and delights of city life that her friend had described for her. So the next day when the Town Mouse asked the Country Mouse to go home with her to the city, she gladly said yes.

When they reached the mansion in which the Town Mouse lived, they found on the table in the dining room the leavings of a very fine banquet. There were sweetmeats and jellies, pastries, delicious cheeses, indeed, the most tempting foods that a Mouse can imagine. But just as the Country Mouse was about to nibble a dainty bit of pastry, she heard a Cat mew loudly and scratch at the door. In great fear the Mice scurried to a hiding place, where they lay quite still for a long time, hardly daring to breathe. When at last they ventured back to the feast, the door opened suddenly and in came the servants to clear the table, followed by the House Dog.

The Country Mouse stopped in the Town Mouse's den only long enough to pick up her carpet bag and umbrella.

"You may have luxuries and dainties that I have not," she said as she hurried away, "but I prefer my plain food and simple life in the country with the peace and security that go with it."

Poverty with security is better than plenty in the midst of fear and uncertainty.

Lesson 6

Read and discuss the quotation.

> *"We never repent of having eaten too little."* — *Thomas Jefferson*

Activity: Role play what to do if someone (a friend or sibling) is urging you to overindulge in something.

Lesson 7

Discuss these Scriptures in relation to Self-Restraint in Indulgences.

Ecclesiastes 7:3, 4—The heart of fools desires constant fun.
Ephesians 5:18—Do not get drunk on wine.
Hebrews 11:24–27—Moses chose to endure mistreatment rather than enjoy the pleasures of sin.

Lesson 8

Read and discuss "The Dog and His Master's Dinner." When you begin to entertain temptation, you're on the edge of giving in. There's a saying that you can't stop a bird from flying over your head, but you can keep it from making a nest in your hair. Throw your attention to your duty, your hobby,—anything but the temptation.

The Dog and His Master's Dinner
from *The Aesop for Children* by Milo Winter

A Dog had learned to carry his master's dinner to him every day. He was very faithful to his duty, though the smell of the good things in the basket tempted him.

The Dogs in the neighborhood noticed him carrying the basket and soon discovered what was in it. They made several attempts to steal it from him. But he always guarded it faithfully.

Then one day all the Dogs in the neighborhood got together and met him on his way with the basket. The Dog tried to run away from them. But at last he stopped to argue.

That was his mistake. They soon made him feel so ridiculous that he dropped the basket and seized a large piece of roast meat intended for his master's dinner.

"Very well," he said, "you divide the rest."

Do not stop to argue with temptation.

Lesson 9

Read and discuss the quotation below.

> *"It is the great curse of Gluttony that it ends by destroying all sense of the precious, the unique, the irreplaceable." — Dorothy Sayers*

Activity: Self-restraint doesn't mean totally keeping away from food or sleep or pleasure. It means going the correct distance and no further. Play a game to illustrate this. Set up several "boundaries" in a line progressing from close to far away, with each boundary several feet from the next. You can designate the boundaries with plastic cups or blocks or lines of tape. Assign points to each boundary, with the most points being the closest one and least points being the farthest one. Each person rolls a ball or puck and tries to get it to end on a boundary that will gain the most points. Continue taking turns for 5 or so rounds and see who gets the most points.

An alternate activity could be to bake some cookies for different lengths of time. Some should be under baked, some baked just right, and some burnt. Let the children sample each cookie and talk about the wisdom of "just right" in indulgences.

Lesson 10

Discontentment can lead to over-indulgence, which still does not satisfy. Read and discuss "The Fisherman and His Wife."

The Fisherman and His Wife
from *Fairy Stories and Fables* by James Baldwin

A Fisherman and his wife lived in a hut close by the sea. They were very poor. The man used to go out in his boat all day to catch fish; and he would fish, and fish, and fish.

Some days he caught all that he and his wife could eat; some days he caught more, and then they had fish to sell; and some days he caught none at all.

One day as he sat in his boat, with his fishing rod in his hand, and gazed at the sea, he felt his line pulled. He drew it up, and there was a fine large fish fast on the hook.

"Please put me back! please put me back!" said the fish.

"Why so?" said the fisherman.

"I am not a real fish," said the fish. "I may look like one, but I am a prince that has been bewitched. Please put me back and let me go."

"Of course I'll put you back," said the man. "I don't want to eat a fish that can talk. I would rather have no dinner at all."

Then he took the fish off the hook and threw it back into the sea. There was a long streak of blood in the water behind it as it sank out of sight. The fisherman gazed into the sea awhile, and then went home in his boat.

"Did you catch any fish to-day?" said his wife.

"Only one," he said. "I caught a fine large one, but it said that it was a prince, and so I threw it back into the sea."

"Did you ask it for anything?" said the woman.

"No," said the man. "What would I ask of a fish?"

"You might have asked it for a nice little cottage," she said. "It is hard to have to live all our lives in a wretched hut like this."

"Ask a fish for a cottage?" said he. "Do you think it would give us one?"

"Certainly," said she. "Have you never heard the song,

" 'Ask anything of a talking fish,
And he will give you what you wish'?

"Now get into your boat and go and call him; say that we want a neat little cottage with three rooms, and a vine climbing over the door."

The man did not like to go back at all; but his wife kept talking and talking till at last he got into his boat and rowed away.

When he came to the place where he had caught the fish, the sea was green and dark, and not bright and clear as it had been before. He stood up in his boat and sang:—

"Once a prince, but now a fish,
Come and listen to my wish.
Come! for my wife, Nancy Bell,
Wishes what I fear to tell."

All at once the fish stuck his head up out of the water and said, "Well, what is it you want?"

"I don't want anything," said the man. "But my wife wants a neat cottage with three rooms, and a vine climbing up over the door."

"Go home," said the fish. "She shall have it."

The man turned his boat and rowed back home; and there was his wife sitting on a bench in front of a neat little cottage. She took him by the hand and said, "Come in, come in. See how much better this is than the dirty hut which we had." They went in and looked at the pretty sitting room and the cozy bedroom, and the kitchen with everything in it that anybody could want. And outside was a yard with chickens and ducks running about, and a little garden full of good things to eat.

"Isn't this nice?" said the wife.

"Yes," said the man, "and we will live here and be happy all our lives."

"We'll think about it," said his wife.

All went very well for three or four weeks. Then the woman began to find fault with things. The house was too small for her, and so were the yard and the garden.

"How I should like to be a fine lady, and live in a great stone castle," she said.

"This cottage is good enough for me," said the man.

"It may be good enough for you," said she, "but it is not good enough for me. Go back to the fish and tell him to give us a great stone castle with high walls and towers."

"I don't like to go," said he. "The fish gave us the cottage, and he might not like it if we asked him for something else."

"He won't care," said the wife. "Go and ask him at once. I cannot bear to live in this little house another day. Go!"

The man got into his boat and rowed slowly away. When he came to the place where he had caught the fish, he stood up and sang:—

"Once a prince, but now a fish,
Come and listen to wife's wish.
Come! for my dear Nancy Bell
Wishes what I fear to tell."

"Well, what does she want now?" asked the fish.

"I like the cottage best," said the man; "but she wants to live in a great stone castle."

"A great stone castle it is," said the fish. "Go home. She is standing at the door, waiting for you."

So the fisherman turned his boat and rowed back home; and there, close by the sea, was a great stone castle; and a very fine lady who looked like his wife was standing at the door.

She took him by the hand, and they went in; and there was a broad hall with a marble floor; and up stairs and down, there were fine rooms with tables and chairs all covered with gold; and crowds of servants stood around ready to wait upon them; and the big table in the dining hall was loaded with food and drink such as they had never heard of before. After dinner the man and woman walked out to see their stables, and fine gardens, and the great park where were deer and hares and everything anybody could want.

"Isn't this grand?" said the wife.

"Yes," said the man, "and we will live and be happy all our lives."

"We'll think about it," said his wife.

All went well till the next morning. The wife woke up first and looked out of the window at the fine country which lay around the castle.

"Husband, get up!" she said. "Get up, and look out of the window. I wish I was the king of all this land."

"Why so?" said her husband. "I think we are well enough off as we are. I don't want to be king."

"Well, but I want to be king," said the wife. "Go back to the fish and tell him so."

The fisherman did not like to go. "It is not right! It is not right!" he said.

But his wife said, "Go at once!"

So he got into his boat and rowed away. When he came to the place where he had caught the fish, he stood up and sang:—

"Once a prince, but now a fish,
Come and listen to wife's wish.
Come! for lady Nancy Bell
Wishes what I fear to tell."

"Well, what does she want now?" said the fish.

"I am ashamed to tell you," said the man; "but she wants to be king."

"Go home," said the fish; "she has her wish."

The fisherman turned his boat and rowed back home. When he got to the shore he saw that the castle was much larger than before; and there were sentinels at the gates, and crowds of soldiers were marching back and forth, and there was a great noise of drums and trumpets. Inside of the castle everything was of silver and gold; and in the great hall was his wife sitting on a throne of ivory and pearls. She had a crown of gold on her head, and many fine ladies and gentlemen stood around her.

"Isn't this glorious?" said she.

"Yes," said the man. "Now we have nothing else to wish for."

"I don't know about that," said his wife.

"But you will be satisfied now, won't you, wife?" he said.

"No, indeed, I will not," she said.

That night she lay in bed, thinking and thinking, and wishing that there was something else she could have. The fisherman slept well and soundly, for he had done a good deal of work that day, rowing his boat back and forth. But his wife turned from one side to the other the whole night through, and did not sleep a wink. At last the sun began to rise, and when she saw the red light come in at her window, she thought: "Ha! how I should like to be the master of the sun!"

Then she shook her husband and said, "Get up! Get up! Go out to the fish and tell him that I want to be the master of the sun."

The fisherman was so frightened that he fell out of the bed. Then he rubbed his eyes and said: "What did you say, wife?"

"I want to be the master of the sun," she said. "I want to make it rise when I choose, and set when I choose, and stand still when I choose."

"Oh, wife," said the man, all in a tremble, "do you want to be a god?"

"That's just what I want to be," she said. "Go out to the fish and tell him so."

"You'd better let well enough alone," said the man. "You are king now; let us be contented!"

This made the woman very angry. She pushed him with her foot, and screamed: "I will not be contented! I will not be contented! Go, and do as I bid you!"

So the man hurried away to his boat. He tried to row out to his fishing place, but a great storm came up, and the waves were so high that he could not see which way to go. The sky was black as ink, and the thunder rolled, and the lightning flashed, and the winds blew terribly. So he shouted as loud as he could:—

> "Once a prince, but now a fish,
> Come and listen to wife's wish.
> Come! for king Nancy Bell
> Wishes what I fear to tell."

"Well, what does she want now?" said the fish.

"She wants—she wants to be the master of the sun," said the man, in a whisper.

"She wants to be a god, does she?" said the fish.

"Ah, yes! That is what she wants to be," said the man.

"Go home, then," said the fish. "You will find her in the poor little dirty hut by the sea."

And there the fisherman and his wife are living to this day.

Lesson 11

Have a Parent Share moment to share a story from your life or tell about a person who exemplifies Self-Restraint in Indulgences.

Lesson 12

Finish up with any other discussion, ideas, or celebration your family enjoys. Keep up this habit while going forth to concentrate on a new one.

Training the Ear and Voice
Hearing and pronouncing words accurately

Parent Prep

Read detailed thoughts about Training the Ear and Voice on pages 145 and 146 of *Laying Down the Rails* and skim the lessons below.

♦ Goals for this Habit (and steps to get there)

_____

_____

_____

♦ A Person or Story from My Life that Demonstrates this Habit

_____

_____

_____

♦ Additional Stories, Poems, Quotations, Bible Verses I Want to Use

_____

_____

_____

♦ Other Activities We Could Do to Practice this Habit

_____

_____

_____

♦ Celebration Ideas

_____

_____

_____

Lesson 1

Read the definition and discuss Training the Ear and Voice. Share with the children any goals you've identified for this habit (for instance, "We will listen closely to the names of those introduced to us and do our best to pronounce them correctly the very first time."). Also get their input on changes they think need to be made.

Read the Biblical principle found in 1 Corinthians 14:7–9 from your preferred version of the Bible. Paul emphasized the importance of speaking words in a manner that listeners could understand them. We cannot use words to minister to others if they cannot understand what we are saying.

Lesson 2

Discuss point two together.

 2. Make a game of pronouncing difficult words precisely after a single hearing.

Activity: Find unfamiliar words (*imperturbability, ipecacuanha, Antananarivo* are examples from Charlotte) and names (Greek names and Biblical names work well) and make a game as suggested by Charlotte of pronouncing difficult words precisely after a single hearing. There are great pronunciation guides online which sometimes include an audible pronunciation.

Point 1. Require your child to pronounce vowel sounds correctly, and don't allow him to leave off final consonants of words.

Lesson 3

Talk over point three. You might use some words from a current foreign language study to practice this habit. Read and discuss the story below.

3. Oral foreign language study is a way to reinforce ear and voice training.

Remind your children that this habit is not an opportunity to show off our own skills so much as an opportunity to encourage others. When we pronounce a person's name correctly or speak a word in someone's language, we are showing respect to them and ministering to them.

Demosthenes the Greatest Orator of Athens
from *The Story of Greece* by Mary Macgregor

Demosthenes had spoken in the law courts, but he was not content. His great ambition now was to speak in the assembly of Athens. He wished to remind the Athenians of their glorious past, he wished to encourage them to fight against the enemies of their country.

His first attempt was a failure. His voice was weak, his sentences long, and before he had finished what he wished to say, the people were laughing and jeering, so that he was forced to sit down.

As he left the assembly he was so unhappy that he thought he would never speak to the people again. He walked along the streets, scarcely knowing, in his distress, where he went.

Suddenly he felt some one touch his arm, and looking up he saw a very old man who had been in the assembly and had heard him speak. He had seen how disappointed Demosthenes was as he left the hall, and he had determined to encourage him. So first he praised the crestfallen orator, saying that his speech had reminded him of the great orator Pericles, and then he upbraided the young man for being so easily discouraged by the laughter of the people.

Demosthenes allowed himself to be comforted and made up his mind to try again, thinking that perhaps after all he would be able to make the people listen to him. But in spite of all his efforts he could not hold their attention, and he left the assembly, hiding his face in his cloak that none might see his sorrow.

An actor, named Satyrus, who knew him well, followed him home, for he guessed that Demosthenes would be in despair. The orator did not hide his trouble from his friend. "The citizens will listen to anyone, even to those who have not studied, rather than to me," he said in bitter anger. "A sailor with a foolish story will make them applaud, while if I tell them tales of the glorious deeds of their own countrymen they pay no heed."

 Habit points from *Laying Down the Rails*

"You say true, Demosthenes," answered Satyrus, "but I will soon tell you how this is if you will recite to me some lines from one of our great poets."

Demosthenes did as his friend asked. But although he said the words correctly, his voice was dull and his attitude was stiff and awkward.

Satyrus said nothing when his friend ended, but himself began to repeat the same lines. Yet you would scarcely have known that they were the same, for the eyes of the actor flashed, his voice rang clear, then sank to a whisper, his body swayed now this way, now that, as he sought to make the meaning of the poem plain.

Then Demosthenes understood as he had never done before how it was that his carefully studied speeches did not interest the Athenians. He must not only read or recite them, he must act them, so that the things of which he spoke might become real to those who listened.

From that day Demosthenes began to work in a different way. He made one of the cellars of his house into a study, that there, undisturbed, he might practise his voice and gestures. He stayed in this strange study for two or three months at a time, and lest he should be tempted to go to theatres or games, he shaved one side of his head, "that so for shame he might not go abroad, though he desired it ever so much."

At other times to strengthen his voice he would go to the seashore while a storm was raging, and putting pebbles in his mouth he would try to make his words heard above the roar of the waves. He also recited speeches while he was out of breath from running up some steep hill, and at home he would stand before a large mirror to watch his gestures and the expression of his face.

And his hard work and perseverance were rewarded, for Demosthenes became what he most desired to be, the greatest orator of Athens. His enemies learned to fear his speeches, his friends to count upon them to aid their cause.

Demosthenes was thirty-three years of age when he made his first speech against Philip of Macedon, who now, in 356 B.C., invaded Greece.

The king would gladly have made an alliance with the Athenians and gained their goodwill. But they, wishing to recover Amphipolis, which he had taken from them, refused to make peace.

Demosthenes lost no opportunity to speak against Philip. He reminded his countrymen that the king was "not the man to rest content with that he has subdued, but is always adding to his conquests, and casts his snare around us while we sit at home postponing." In another speech he told the Athenians that they chose their captains, "not to fight, but to be displayed like dolls in the market-place."

These and other speeches against the king of Macedon were called "The Philippics" of Demosthenes, and still today, if someone makes a speech against a special person, although his name is not Philip, we call the speech a "Philippic."

Lesson 4

Nonsense poetry and literature can have unusual words and pronunciation. It's fun to read, and it's even better if it is read without stutters and stops. Have fun taking turns trying to recite or read portions of "Eletelephany" precisely.

Eletelephany
by Laura Richards

Once there was an elephant,
Who tried to use the telephant—
No! No! I mean an elephone

Who tried to use the telephone—
(Dear me! I am not certain quite
That even now I've got it right.)

Howe'er it was, he got his trunk
Entangled in the telephunk;
The more he tried to get it free,
The louder buzzed the telephee—
(I fear I'd better drop the song
Of elephop and telephong!)

Lesson 5

Talk about the different accents or dialects that one language can have.

Read Judges 12:4–6. In the midst of a war with the Ephraimites, anyone who tried to cross the Jordan River had to first pronounce the word "Shibboleth" to the guards. If they pronounced it with the peculiar accent of the Ephraimites, their true identity was exposed.

Lesson 6

Pronouncing foreign names can be a great benefit when communicating with those from other countries.

Activity: Let the children make up unusual names and introduce themselves to a sibling with a handshake. The sibling should respond with their own name and say, "Nice to meet you _____," pronouncing the name correctly the first time. You might be able to befriend a family from a different country or get involved in a refugee community and put this training to good use.

Lesson 7

Take the time you need to listen and practice so that you can speak distinctly and pleasantly. Read and discuss "The Singing Bird."

The Singing Bird
from *Harper's Third Reader*, edited by James Baldwin

Bessie and George and Grace had a bird given them in a fine large cage. It was a canary, young and very tame.

While the weather was fine the children kept their bird out in their own little summerhouse in the garden. There they spent much of their time, talking to it and trying to make it still more tame.

One day George said: "Come, sisters, I have thought of a plan to please mother. She has never heard our bird sing, and I think that I can teach him to warble that pretty Indian air which she likes so well. If I can do this, we will hang Dicky up at her window, early on her birthday, and he will wake her with the song."

Bessie and Grace liked this plan very much, and George began to give lessons to the bird. He played very slowly on his fife the air which they wished Dicky to learn. This he did three or four times every day.

But Dicky was very naughty. Sometimes he would sit quietly with his feathers stuck out like a frill, and his head on one side, looking very cross. Sometimes he would hop about the cage eating his food and seeming not to notice George.

George, with great patience, played the tune over and over again. At the end Dicky would give a sort of a little chirp, as much as to say, Ah!—and that was all.

At other times he would sing his own song—sweet enough, to be sure, but not the one they wanted. George began to feel vexed, and the children were almost ready to give up their plan.

"He will never learn it," said little Grace, one day. "It is now only a week till mother's birthday, and he has never sung a note of the tune."

"Hush!" said Bessie; "here it comes, I do believe."

But no! Dicky sat as still as a mouse, turning his head to one side, in the most cunning way you could think of.

The next day, as the children were in the garden, they heard the air which they loved, warbled in a low, sweet strain in the summerhouse!

"He knows it at last!" cried George. "The little fellow has only been waiting till he could sing it well!"

And it seemed as if this were true; for from that moment Dicky warbled away at the pretty air as if he knew no sweeter song. On the morning of their mother's birthday they had the pleasure of seeing her delight when she was awakened by the Indian air sung by little Dicky.

Lesson 8

Have a Parent Share moment to share a story from your life or tell about a person who exemplifies Training of Ear and Voice, then read and discuss the quotation below.

> *"Speak properly, and in as few words as you can, but always plainly; for the end of speech is not ostentation, but to be understood."* — *William Penn*

Lesson 9

Finish up with any other discussion, ideas, or celebration your family enjoys. Keep up this habit while going forth to concentrate on a new one.

Religious Habits

Regularity in Devotions

Having a personal time of prayer, praise, and Bible reading

Parent Prep

Read detailed thoughts about Regularity in Devotions on pages 148–152 of *Laying Down the Rails*.

Contemplate for yourself first, and then talk over these points with your children before delving into Prayer, Praise, and Bible Reading.

■ 1. Communicate the importance of daily devotions by word and example.

■ 2. Establish a set time and place for daily devotions.

■ 3. Be sure to schedule an unhurried time for devotions when your child is fully awake and alert.

■ 4. A well-chosen devotional book can be a good supplement to your child's devotional time.

■ 7. Teach your child that, though devotions are very helpful to us, his having devotions does not earn him merit with God.

Charlotte wrote directly to young people about knowledge of God, prayer, thanksgiving, praise, and faith in Volume 4, Book 2, pages 174–202.

■ Habit points from *Laying Down the Rails*

Prayer

Parent Prep

Skim the lessons below.

    ♦ Goals for this Habit (and steps to get there)

_____

_____

_____

    ♦ A Person or Story from My Life that Demonstrates this Habit

_____

_____

_____

    ♦ Additional Stories, Poems, Quotations, Bible Verses I Want to Use

_____

_____

_____

    ♦ Other Activities We Could Do to Practice this Habit

_____

_____

_____

    ♦ Celebration Ideas

_____

_____

_____

With all the prompting for discussion, be careful not to overtalk. Encourage the children to chime in and give their thoughts and ask questions.

Lesson 1

Discuss Prayer. Share with the children any goals you've identified for this habit (for instance, "We will include prayer in our morning routine and at night before bedtime, while encouraging spontaneous prayer as well."). Also get their input on changes they think need to be made.

Read the Biblical principle found in 1 Timothy 2:1, 2, and 8 from your preferred version of the Bible. The Bible is full of examples of Prayer and encouragement to pray.

Lesson 2

Discuss point five and the poem together.

5. Remember both spontaneous prayer and set times of purposeful prayer.

As Down in the Sunless Retreats
by Thomas Moore

As down in the sunless retreats of the ocean
Sweet flowers are springing no mortal can see,
So deep in my soul the still prayer of devotion,
Unheard by the world, rises silent to Thee.

Remember that you can use quotations or poems for copywork or recitation lessons.

Lesson 3

Read and discuss the quotation below.

"There is nothing that makes us love someone so much as praying for them." — *William Law*

Activity: Create a family Prayer Album. Put in photos of extended family members and friends, one per page. Each day turn to the next photo page, tell who that person is, and pray for them. Share appropriate details or prayer requests as you keep in contact with those people.

Lesson 4

Faithfulness in Prayer is a rare and beautiful gift to develop. It is fragrant to God and a blessing to fellow man.

Read Daniel chapter 6. Daniel continued his regular prayer times at his open window in spite of opposition and threat of death.

Lesson 5

Prayer helps us see our place in relationship to God. It humbles us to acknowledge God as He is and realize our lowly position as humans. He is Creator; we are creation. Read and discuss the poem, "Strong Son of God, Immortal Love."

Strong Son of God, Immortal Love
by Alfred, Lord Tennyson

Strong Son of God, immortal Love,
   Whom we, that have not seen Thy face,
   By faith, and faith alone, embrace,
Believing where we cannot prove;

Thine are these orbs of light and shade;
   Thou madest Life in man and brute;
   Thou madest Death; and lo, thy foot
Is on the skull which Thou has made.

Habit points from
Laying Down the Rails

Thou wilt not leave us in the dust:
 Thou madest man, he knows not why;
 He thinks he was not made to die;
Thou Thou hast made him: Thou art just.

Thou seemest human and divine,
 The highest, holiest manhood, Thou.
 Our wills are ours, we know not how;
Ours wills are ours, to make them Thine.

Our little systems have their day;
 They have their day and cease to be:
 They are but broken lights of Thee,
And Thou, O Lord, art more than they.

We have but faith: we cannot know;
 For knowledge is of things we see;
 And yet we trust it comes from Thee,
A beam in darkness: let it grow.

Let knowledge grow from more to more,
 But more of reverence in us dwell;
 That mind and soul, according well,
May make one music as before,

But vaster. We are fools and slight;
 We mock Thee when we do not fear:
 But help Thy foolish ones to bear;
Help Thy vain worlds to bear Thy light.

Lesson 6

God is a real Being Who listens to our prayers. Share together examples of answered prayers.

Activity: Read Scriptures that give pictures of God dwelling in Heaven; for example, Isaiah 6:1–5 or Revelation chapter 4. Have the children picture God upon His throne and let them describe the scenes to you. Help them remember this picture of God each time they pray so that God becomes a real Being to them and they don't simply pray with no thought as to Who is listening.

Lesson 7

We have direct access to our Father in Heaven at any time and place. Read and discuss "The Light that is Felt."

The Light that is Felt
by John Greenleaf Whittier

A tender child of summers three,

Seeking her little bed at night,
Paused on the dark stair timidly.
"Oh, mother! Take my hand," said she,
"And then the dark will all be light."

We older children grope our way
From dark behind to dark before;
And only when our hands we lay,
Dear Lord, in Thine, the night is day,
And there is darkness nevermore.

Reach downward to the sunless days
Wherein our guides are blind as we,
And faith is small and hope delays;
Take Thou the hands of prayer we raise,
And let us feel the light of Thee!

Lesson 8

Our prayers are meant to be direct communication with a loving Father, not moments that boost our ego and turn attention to us.

Read Matthew 6:5–15, "The Lord's Prayer" and instruction on how to pray.

Lesson 9

Have a Parent Share moment to share a story from your life or tell about a person who exemplifies a habit of Prayer, then read and discuss the quotation below. Make sure children recognize John Bunyan as the author of *The Pilgrim's Progress*.

> *"You can do more than pray after you have prayed, but you cannot do more than pray until you have prayed." — John Bunyan*

Lesson 10

There are moments when we realize God is the only One we can turn to. And He stands ready to help, even if we had no thought of Him before. The following poem is especially good for older children.

Prayer in the Time of War
by Alfred Noyes

Thou, whose deep ways are in the sea,
Whose footsteps are not known,
Tonight a world that turned from Thee
Is waiting—at Thy Throne.

The towering Babels that we raised
Where scoffing sophists brawl,
The little Antichrists we praised—
The night is on them all.

> *The fool hath said . . . The fool hath said . . .*
>   And we, who deemed him wise,
>   We who believed that Thou wast dead,
>   How should we seek Thine eyes?
>
>   How should we seek to Thee for power
>   Who scorned Thee yesterday?
>   How should we kneel, in this dread hour?
>   Lord, teach us how to pray!
>
>   Grant us the single heart, once more,
>   That mocks no sacred thing,
>   The Sword of Truth our fathers wore
>   When Thou wast Lord and King.
>
>   Let darkness unto darkness tell
>   Our deep unspoken prayer,
>   For, while our souls in darkness dwell,
>   We know that Thou art there.

Lesson 11

Jesus had times alone in prayer.

Read Mark 1:35, Mark 6:45 and 46, and Luke 5:15 and 16.

Lesson 12

Read and discuss the quotation.

> *"Prayer . . . the key of the day and the lock of the night."* — *Thomas Fuller*

Activity: Let the children practice praying out loud. There are any number of creative ways to pray:

- ♦ Popcorn prayer (Anyone can pray at any time as long as you do not interrupt or talk at the same time as another. Spoken prayers can be any length, and anyone may pray as often as desired during the time.)
- ♦ Chain prayer (One person starts the prayer, the next person adds on, and so on down the line until the last person ends the prayer.)
- ♦ Follow the ACTS acronym: Adoration, Confession, Thanksgiving, Supplication.
- ♦ Follow the pattern of the Lord's Prayer (Matthew 6:9–13).
- ♦ Use a map to pray for other countries and peoples who need to hear about the one true God and His Son, Jesus Christ.
- ♦ Pray over pictures of special people in your life.
- ♦ Try a different posture: kneeling, raising hands, folding hands, or holding hands.
- ♦ Appoint a daily prayer person who prays at meals and at bedtime or devotion time.
- ♦ Choose Scriptures to pray, such as a Psalm (Many of them are written as prayers.) or any Scripture you have read that day. For example, if you read 1 John 2, you might choose a few verses from that chapter to turn into a prayer,

such as, "Thank you for giving us Jesus who speaks in our defense when we sin. Help us to walk as Jesus walked and to love You by obeying You."

Lesson 13

Talk about different aspects of Prayer using the following Scriptures:

Ephesians 6:18–20—Pray with all kinds of prayers and requests.
Colossians 4:2–4—Devote yourself to prayer.
1 Thessalonians 5:16, 17—Pray continually.
James 5:13–18—The prayer of a righteous man is powerful.

Lesson 14

Finish up with any other discussion, ideas, or celebration your family enjoys. Keep up this habit while going forth to concentrate on a new one.

Notes

Reading the Bible

Parent Prep

Skim the lessons below.

♦ Goals for this Habit (and steps to get there)

_____

_____

_____

♦ A Person or Story from My Life that Demonstrates this Habit

_____

_____

_____

♦ Additional Stories, Poems, Quotations, Bible Verses I Want to Use

_____

_____

_____

♦ Other Activities We Could Do to Practice this Habit

_____

_____

_____

♦ Celebration Ideas

_____

_____

_____

📖6. Give your child plenty of direct contact with the Bible itself, not watered down re-tellings, and select those passages that are appropriate for children.

Lesson 1

Discuss Reading the Bible. Share with the children any goals you've identified for this habit (for instance, "Every member of the family will own a personal Bible so they can read it at any time."). Also get their input on changes they think need to be made.

Read the Biblical principle found in Psalm 1:1 and 2 from your preferred version of the Bible. The righteous person delights in meditating on God's law day and night.

Lesson 2

Some people groups do not have the Bible in their own language or are not allowed to own or read the Bible. Consider the privilege we have to own several copies of God's Word—and not only own them, but have the ability to read them.

📖 Habit points from Laying Down the Rails

Activity: If your children do not have their own Bibles, you could make a special trip to purchase a Bible with them. You could also let them pick out a journal or special pen, or they may need an alarm clock to aid in getting themselves up earlier to have personal daily Bible reading. The Bible is a treasure. Treat the acquiring of a Bible as you would if you acquired a pearl necklace or expensive car. Celebrate it and teach them how to handle a Bible respectfully.

Lesson 3

God's Word is life-giving. You may not be aware of its absence until you hear it again, and then you realize you were hot and dusty and in need of the cool drink of water that refreshed your soul.

Read Nehemiah chapter 8. The people wept and rejoiced when they finally got to hear and understand the Law of the Lord.

Lesson 4

A routine time for Bible reading ensures that the Word of God is regularly heard. There are different types of Bible reading: reading through the Bible for knowledge of God and His ways, studying the Bible for deeper insight and connection, and pondering shorter sections for meditation. Read and discuss this excerpt from *The Hiding Place*.

from *The Hiding Place*
by Corrie ten Boom
Fleming H. Revell Company, 1974, pages 7 and 8

"Father stood up and took the big brass-hinged Bible from its shelf as Toos and Hans rapped on the door and came in. Scripture reading at 8:30 each morning for all who were in the house was another of the fixed points around which life in the Beje revolved. Father opened the big volume and Betsie and I held our breaths. Surely, today of all days, when there was still so much to do, it would not be a whole chapter! But he was turning to the Gospel of Luke where we'd left off yesterday—such long chapters in Luke too. With his finger at the place, Father looked up.

'Where is Christoffels?' he said.

. . . For the first time, Christoffels was late. Father polished his glasses with his napkin and started to read, his deep voice lingering lovingly over the words. He had reached the bottom of the page when we heard Christoffels' shuffling steps on the stairs. The door opened and all of us gasped. Christoffels was resplendent in a new black suit, new checkered vest, a snowy white shirt, flowered tie, and stiff starched collar. I tore my eyes from the spectacle as swiftly as I could, for Christoffels' expression forbade us to notice anything out of the ordinary.

'Christoffels, my dear associate,' Father murmured in his formal, old-fashioned way, 'what joy to see you on this—er—auspicious day.' And hastily he resumed his Bible reading."

One action done to practice a habit does not mean you have accomplished that habit. Repeated action helps you sharpen your skills so you will naturally be ready to use your habit when the need arises in life.

Lesson 5

Read and discuss the quotation. Make sure the children know who Moody was.

"The Bible will keep you from sin, or sin will keep you from the Bible." — *D. L. Moody*

Activity: Create a Bible reading schedule that is doable for each child. Get an audio Bible for those who cannot read yet.

Lesson 6

We can trust the Bible to be true and steadfast. It is the standard to which we compare our lives to see what we need to change in ourselves. Read and discuss the poem below.

The Mirror
by Phoebe Law

I go to the mirror and comb my hair
The way I'd like it to go.
But when I go outside it doesn't look nice
When the wind begins to blow.

I go to the Bible, the mirror of God
And like the one on the wall,
I behold what manner of man I should be
Then straightway forget and fall.

This mirror reflects in minute detail
Each thought I keep in my heart,
It searches the motives for the things I do
And pulls and tears them apart.

Satan would have us defeated to be
Each battle we fail to win,
But if we return to God's mirror each time
We still can find peace within.

And so it is as we travel through life,
We may choose to do quite well,
But as we look back, we're forced to admit
How often we've slipped and fell.

We must not give up, we must walk by faith
Tis true we'll stumble some more.
But God's mirror reflects that this is the way
The faithful have walked before.

Lesson 7

God's complete plan is not meant to cause hopeless guilt. The Bible points out our sin, but it also shows that His plan provides a way for repentance, forgiveness, and the hope of Heaven.

Read 2 Chronicles chapter 34. Josiah, a young king of Judah, began to seek God and tear down the idols around the country. He had the temple cleaned and the Book of the Law was found. Repentance was his reaction to the Word.

Lesson 8

Read and discuss the quotation.

> *"Unless we form the habit of going to the Bible in bright moments as well as in trouble, we cannot fully respond to its consolations because we lack equilibrium between light and darkness." — Helen Keller*

Activity: Let the readers in your home practice reading a section of Scripture out loud. Model for them first how to read with expression, interest, and distinctness and not in a monotone voice. After the Scripture has been read, ask one or two probing questions to get them to think or have them narrate the text. The family could journal their thoughts and questions as well. Challenge the older children to commit to reading through a book of the Bible on their own within a time period (two weeks, for example).

Lesson 9

The Bible is life for those who obey it but foolishness to those who are callous toward it.

Read Psalm 119:65–72 and Hebrews 4:12. The Word of God is active, convicting and healing.

Whether reading or reciting aloud, be sure to reflect the life that is in God's Word!

Lesson 10

Have a Parent Share moment to share a story from your life or tell about a person who exemplifies this habit of Reading the Bible.

Finish up with any other discussion, ideas, or celebration your family enjoys. Keep up this habit while going forth to concentrate on a new one.

Praise

Parent Prep

Skim the lessons below.

♦ Goals for this Habit (and steps to get there)

_____

_____

_____

♦ A Person or Story from My Life that Demonstrates this Habit

_____

_____

_____

♦ Additional Stories, Poems, Quotations, Bible Verses I Want to Use

_____

_____

_____

♦ Other Activities We Could Do to Practice this Habit

_____

_____

_____

♦ Celebration Ideas

_____

_____

_____

Lesson 1

Discuss Praise. Share with the children any goals you've identified for this habit (for instance, "We will think about the words we read, say, or sing when we are praising God."). Also get their input on changes they think need to be made.

Read the Biblical principle found in Isaiah 25:1 from your preferred version of the Bible.

God is exalted above all mankind, above all creation. There are many attributes of God for which we can praise Him; Isaiah mentions faithfulness, marvelous things He has done, and foreknowledge and planning.

Lesson 2

Discuss point eight. Praise can be written, spoken in prayer, read from Scripture, or listened to/sung using praise music. Read and discuss "Caedmon's Hymn."

 8. Make praise an integral part of your daily devotions.

Caedmon's Hymn

Now let me praise the keeper of Heaven's kingdom,
The might of the Creator, and His thought,
The work of the Father of glory, how each of wonders
The Eternal Lord established in the beginning.
He first created for the sons of men
Heaven as a roof, the holy Creator,
Then Middle-earth the keeper of mankind,
The Eternal Lord, afterwards made,
The earth for men, the Almighty Lord.

You can read more about Caedmon's story in Lesson 10 on Fortitude on page 328.

Lesson 3

Talk about point nine.

Read and discuss the quotation. make sure the children know who Spurgeon was.

"God is to be praised with the voice, and the heart should go therewith in holy exultation." — Charles H. Spurgeon

 9. Sing hymns and other worship songs reverently, offering your best praise.

Activity: Listen to and sing praise songs or hymns of praise. Teach your children how to act during praise time and also to think about the words they are singing so as not to get in the habit of empty worship.

Lesson 4

Talk about point ten.

 10. Realize there is a story in the lyrics of hymns.

Activity: Read a hymn and see if young children can find the story. Possible story-hymns could be "One Day," "Tell Me the Story of Jesus," "While Shepherds Watched Their Flocks By Night," "At Calvary," "Jesus Paid It All," or "Love Lifted Me."

Lesson 5

Revelation 4:11 talks about God's being worthy of praise because He created all things. Read and discuss the poem, "The Lamb."

🖼 Habit points from
Laying Down the Rails

The Lamb
by William Blake

Little lamb, who made thee?
Dost thou know who made thee,
Gave thee life, and bid thee feed
By the stream and o'er the mead;
Gave thee clothing of delight,
Softest clothing woolly bright;
Gave thee such a tender voice,
Making all the vales rejoice?
   Little lamb, who made thee?
   Dost thou know who made thee?

Little lamb, I'll tell thee:
Little lamb, I'll tell thee:
He is called by thy name,
For he calls Himself a Lamb.
He is meek and He is mild,
He became a little child.
I a child, and thou a lamb,
We are called by His name.
   Little lamb, God bless thee!
   Little lamb, God bless thee!

Lesson 6

God is worthy of praise no matter our circumstances. There are examples in the Bible of personal praise despite hardships. We should be careful to praise God in good times and bad.

Read Job 1, Psalm 57, or Habakkuk 3:17–19. Despite disaster, these men praised God.

Lesson 7

Praise puts us in a humble frame of mind. Our thoughts are turned toward God instead of toward ourselves.

Activity: Read Psalm 100 or another psalm of praise, such as Psalm 8, 29, 34, 40, 63, 92, 103, or 147.

Lesson 8

There are examples of small groups praising God in the Bible and of corporate praise.

Read Ruth 4:13–17. As the women spoke to Naomi, they praised God for the blessing He brought to her family.

Read 2 Chronicles chapter 5. One example of the Israelites' praising God together is recorded here.

Many good truths about God's character and reasons to praise Him can be found in Bible stories. Allow your children to notice and talk about those also.

Lesson 9

When we live obedient to God, our very lives speak praise of Him. Read and discuss the poem below.

Requirement
by John Greenleaf Whittier

We live by Faith; but Faith is not the slave
   Of text and legend. Reason's voice and God's,
   Nature's and Duty's, never are at odds.
What asks our Father of His children, save
Justice and mercy and humility,
   A reasonable service of good deeds,
   Pure living, tenderness to human needs,
Reverence and trust, and prayer for light to see
The Master's footprints in our daily ways?
   No knotted scourge nor sacrificial knife,
   But the calm beauty of an ordered life
Whose very breathing is unworded praise!—
A life that stands as all true lives have stood,
Firm-rooted in the faith that God is Good.

Lesson 10

Have a Parent Share moment to share a story from your life or tell about a person who exemplifies Praise to God.

Finish up with any other discussion, ideas, or celebration your family enjoys. Keep up this habit while going forth to concentrate on a new one.

Reverent Attitude

Expressing worship in one's demeanor and actions

Parent Prep

Read detailed thoughts about Reverent Attitude on pages 153–155 of *Laying Down the Rails* and skim the lessons below.

+ Goals for this Habit (and steps to get there)

_____

_____

_____

+ A Person or Story from My Life that Demonstrates this Habit

_____

_____

_____

+ Additional Stories, Poems, Quotations, Bible Verses I Want to Use

_____

_____

_____

+ Other Activities We Could Do to Practice this Habit

_____

_____

_____

+ Celebration Ideas

_____

_____

_____

Lesson 1

Read the definition and discuss a Reverent Attitude toward God and the things of God. Share with the children any goals you've identified for this habit (for instance, "We will close our eyes, fold our hands, and concentrate on the words spoken during prayer time."). Also get their input on changes they think need to be made.

Read the Biblical principle found in Titus 2:3 from your preferred version of the Bible. Older women (but the principle can be extrapolated to include everyone) are to be reverent in the way that they live.

Lesson 2

Discuss point one. As with agape love, reverence should be expressed even when we don't feel like it with hopes that reverent feelings will come later as we continue the right actions.

 1. **Reverence is not merely outward conformity, but reverent actions can awaken reverent feelings.**

Activity: The children can create and act out a scene in which someone is meeting a king or president. They should include respect for the person through bowing or kneeling. (You could mention the story of Esther going before the king.) An alternative scene would be to act out proper versus improper behavior for sitting through a church service.

Lesson 3

Talk over point two. Each family member can share what he or she thinks a worshipful demeanor looks like.

 2. **Demonstrate a worshipful demeanor during prayer, whether at meals, at family worship, at personal prayers, or in church.**

Read Luke 2:21–40. Simeon and Anna were blessed to see Jesus while they were alive. Simeon was righteous and devout, and Anna spent her time fasting and praying in the temple.

Lesson 4

Talk about point three. Revelation 4:8–11 gives us a picture of how heavenly creatures show reverence to God as they worship Him. Consider how foolish we must sometimes appear because we forget our God. Read and discuss "King Canute on the Seashore."

 3. **Show as much respect for God as the angels do.**

You can retell Bible stories in your own words instead of reading them straight from the Bible, if you wish. You could also use a Bible storybook for some of the suggested stories.

King Canute on the Seashore
from *Fifty Famous Stories Retold* by James Baldwin

A hundred years or more after the time of Alfred the Great there was a king of England named Canute. King Canute was a Dane; but the Danes were not so fierce and cruel then as they had been when they were at war with King Alfred.

The great men and officers who were around King Canute were always praising him.

"You are the greatest man that ever lived," one would say.

Then another would say, "O king! there can never be another man so mighty as you."

And another would say, "Great Canute, there is nothing in the world that dares to disobey you."

The king was a man of sense, and he grew very tired of hearing such foolish speeches.

One day he was by the seashore, and his officers were with him. They were praising him, as they were in the habit of doing. He thought that now he would teach them a

 Habit points from *Laying Down the Rails*

lesson, and so he bade them set his chair on the beach close by the edge of the water.

"Am I the greatest man in the world?" he asked.

"O king!" they cried, "there is no one so mighty as you."

"Do all things obey me?" he asked.

"There is nothing that dares to disobey you, O king!" they said. "The world bows before you, and gives you honor."

"Will the sea obey me?" he asked; and he looked down at the little waves which were lapping the sand at his feet.

The foolish officers were puzzled, but they did not dare to say "No."

"Command it, O king! and it will obey," said one.

"Sea," cried Canute, "I command you to come no farther! Waves, stop your rolling, and do not dare to touch my feet!"

But the tide came in, just as it always did. The water rose higher and higher. It came up around the king's chair, and wet not only his feet, but also his robe. His officers stood about him, alarmed, and wondering whether he was not mad.

Then Canute took off his crown, and threw it down upon the sand.

"I shall never wear it again," he said. "And do you, my men, learn a lesson from what you have seen. There is only one King who is all-powerful; and it is he who rules the sea, and holds the ocean in the hollow of his hand. It is he whom you ought to praise and serve above all others."

4. Don't assume that actions or postures that demonstrate reverence are tiresome to your child.

5. Allow your young child a quiet and appropriate book or toy to keep his hands busy during the church service, and encourage children of all ages to participate in the parts of the service that they can.

Lesson 5

Discuss point five.

 5. Participate in those parts of the church service that you can.

Read Exodus 20:7, Leviticus 19:12, Isaiah 58:1–5, and Jeremiah 7:9–11. We are to show reverence for God's name. We are not to sin without repentance and then come before God in false reverence, acting as if there is nothing wrong in our lives.

Lesson 6

Ecclesiastes 12:13 talks about the whole duty of man: fear God and obey Him.

Activity: Read Scriptures that show God's holiness, his graciousness, his status as Creator, perhaps his judgment for those who don't choose Him, etc. Let the children form a picture of God that includes all aspects of his character, so that they do not become flippant toward Him. You could print the Scriptures and pass them out for the children to read aloud, or you could spread this activity out over several days, reading one passage per day. You could also make a collage or notebook of God's character traits adding to it as you find new names or traits. Here are some possible passages.

- Isaiah 43 (select sections of verses from this chapter)
- Isaiah 40:25, 26
- Psalm 22:3–5
- Isaiah 6:1–5
- 1 Samuel 2:2
- Psalm 86:15
- Psalm 145
- Exodus 34:6, 7

- Matthew 10:26–39
- Mark 12:38–40
- 1 Chronicles 29:10–13

Lesson 7

Romans 12:9 tells us to hate what is evil and cling to what is good. "The Brave Brethren of Judah" gives us an example of showing ultimate reverence for God.

The Brave Brethren of Judah
adapted from *A Book of Golden Deeds* by Charlotte Yonge

It was about 180 years before the Christian era. The Jews had long since come home from Babylon, and built up their city and Temple at Jerusalem. But they were not free as they had been before. Their country belonged to some greater power, they had a foreign governor over them, and had to pay tribute to the king who was their master.

At the time we are going to speak of, this king was Antiochus Epiphanes, King of Syria. He was descended from one of those generals who, upon the death of Alexander the Great, had shared the East between them, and he reigned over all the country from the Mediterranean Sea even into Persia and the borders of India. He spoke Greek, and believed in both the Greek and Roman gods, for he had spent some time at Rome in his youth; but in his Eastern kingdom he had learnt all the self-indulgent and violent habits to which people in those hot countries are especially tempted.

He was so fierce and passionate, that he was often called the 'Madman', and he was very cruel to all who offended him. One of his greatest desires was, that the Jews should leave their true faith in one God, and do like the Greeks and Syrians, his other subjects, worship the same idols, and hold drunken feasts in their honor. Sad to say, a great many of the Jews had grown ashamed of their own true religion and the strict ways of their law, and thought them old-fashioned. They joined in the Greek sports, played games naked in the theatre, joined in riotous processions, carrying ivy in honor of Bacchus, the god of wine, and offered incense to the idols; and the worst of all these was the false high priest, Menelaus, who led the King Antiochus into the Temple itself, even into the Holy of Holies, and told him all that would most desecrate it and grieve the Jews. So a little altar to the Roman god Jupiter was set up on the top of the great brazen altar of burnt offerings, a hog was offered up, and broth of its flesh sprinkled everywhere in the Temple; then all the precious vessels were seized, the shewbread table of gold, the candlesticks, and the whole treasury, and carried away by the king; the walls were thrown down, and the place made desolate.

Some Jews were still faithful to their God, but they were horribly punished and tortured to death before the eyes of the king; and when at last he went away to his own country, taking with him the wicked high priest Menelaus, he left behind him a governor and an army of soldiers stationed in the tower of Acra, which overlooked the Temple hill, and sent for an old man from Athens to teach the people the heathen rites and ceremonies. Any person who observed the Sabbath day, or any other ordinance of the law of Moses, was put to death in a most cruel manner; all the books of the Old Testament Scripture that could be found were either burnt or defiled, by having pictures of Greek gods painted upon them; and the heathen priests went from place to place, with a little brazen altar and image and a guard of soldiers, who were to kill every person who refused to burn incense before the idol. It was the very saddest time that the Jews had ever known, and there seemed no help near or far off; they could have no hope, except in the promises that God would never fail His people, or forsake His inheritance, and in the prophecies that bad times should come, but good ones after them.

The Greeks, in going through the towns to enforce the idol worship, came to a little city called Modin, somewhere on the hills on the coast of the Mediterranean Sea, not far from Joppa. There they sent out, as usual, orders to all the men of the town to meet them in the marketplace; but they were told beforehand, that the chief person in the place was an old man named Mattathias, of a priestly family, and so much respected, that all the other inhabitants of the place were sure to do whatever he might lead them in. So the Greeks sent for him first of all, and he came at their summons, a grand and noble old man, followed by his five sons, Johanan, Simon, Judas, Jonathan, and Eleazar. The Greek priest tried to talk him over. He told him that the high priest had forsaken the Jewish superstition, that the Temple was in ruins, and that resistance was in vain; and exhorted him to obtain gratitude and honor for himself, by leading his countrymen in thus adoring the deities of the king's choice, promising him rewards and treasures if he would comply. But the old man spoke out with a loud and fearless voice:

'Though all the nations that are under the king's dominion obey him, and fall away every one from the religion of their fathers, and give consent to his commandments; yet will I and my sons and my brethren walk in the covenant of our fathers. God forbid that we should forsake the law and the ordinances! We will not hearken to the king's words, to go from our religion, either on the right hand or the left!'

As he spoke, up came an apostate Jew to do sacrifice at the heathen altar. Mattathias trembled at the sight, and his zeal broke forth. He slew the offender, and his brave sons gathering round him, they attacked the Syrian soldiers, killed the commissioner, and threw down the altar. Then, as they knew that they could not there hold out against the king's power, Mattathias proclaimed throughout the city: 'Whosoever is zealous of the law, and maintaineth the covenant, let him follow me!' With that, he and his five sons, with their families, left their houses and lands, and drove their cattle with them up into the wild hills and caves, where David had once made his home; and all the Jews who wished to be still faithful, gathered around them, to worship God and keep His commandments.

There they were, a handful of brave men in the mountains, and all the heathen world and apostate Jews against them. They used to come down into the villages, remind the people of the law, promise their help, and throw down any idol altars that they found, and the enemy never were able to follow them into their rocky strongholds. But the old Mattathias could not long bear the rude wild life in the cold mountains, and he soon died. First he called all his five sons, and bade them to 'be zealous for the law, and give their lives for the covenant of their fathers'; and he reminded them of all the many brave men who had before served God, and been aided in their extremity. He appointed his son Judas, as the strongest and mightiest, to lead his brethren to battle, and Simon, as the wisest, to be their counsellor; then he blessed them and died; and his sons were able to bury him in the tomb of his fathers at Modin.

Lesson 8

Have a Parent Share moment to share a story from your life or tell about a person who exemplifies Reverent Attitude.

Lesson 9

Reverence begins with a healthy fear of God and obedience to Him.

Read Numbers 4:5, 6, 15 and 2 Samuel 6:1–7. Uzzah showed irreverence by disobeying God's instructions and touching the ark of the covenant. The ark was not moved according to specific plans laid out by God, and death resulted.

Lesson 10

Finish up with any other discussion, ideas, or celebration your family enjoys. Keep up this habit while going forth to concentrate on a new one.

Sunday-Keeping

Setting aside Sunday to focus especially on God and to rest from everyday pursuits

Parent Prep

Read detailed thoughts about Sunday-Keeping on pages 155–157 of *Laying Down the Rails* and skim the lessons below.

♦ Goals for this Habit (and steps to get there)

_____

_____

_____

♦ A Person or Story from My Life that Demonstrates this Habit

_____

_____

_____

♦ Additional Stories, Poems, Quotations, Bible Verses I Want to Use

_____

_____

_____

♦ Other Activities We Could Do to Practice this Habit

_____

_____

_____

♦ Celebration Ideas

_____

_____

_____

The main principle is to set aside one day in seven to rest and especially focus on God. In Charlotte Mason's experience, that was Sunday. If your family sets aside another day of the week to rest, adjust the ideas presented here.

Lesson 1

Read the definition and discuss Sunday-Keeping. Share with the children any goals you've identified for this habit (for instance, "We will spend relaxing time in nature on Sunday afternoons.") Also get their input on changes they think need to be made.

There is no command in the New Testament for a complete day of rest likened to the Sabbath day God commanded for the Old Covenant Israelites. But there is a general principle of taking time to rest and think on God. Acts 20:7 shows the Christians meeting together on Sunday. In Mark 6:30 and 31 Jesus called His disciples to come to a quiet place and rest. And Psalm 143:5 is a great reminder of what should be a consistent practice for all believers: meditating on all God's works.

Lesson 2

Discuss point one, evaluating how your family currently spends Sundays, then discuss the proverb below.

 1. Sunday activities should be special to the day—not rigid or dull, but quiet and glad.

"A Sunday well-spent brings a week of content." — Proverb

Lesson 3

Talk over point two, letting each person describe what he or she enjoys for a change of pace.

 2. A change of pace on Sunday is helpful physically and mentally.

Activity: Think of a fun, relaxing activity that is not a normal part of your week and begin a Sunday family tradition (if you do not already have one). You may need to "try on" several to see what fits your family and schedule. This could be a simple Sunday supper like popcorn or sandwiches. It could be an hour of board games or a hike in nature or an afternoon of resting and reading.

Lesson 4

Read and discuss "The Village Blacksmith," then consider point three.

 3. Sunday activities should promote communion with nature and with God.

The Village Blacksmith
by Henry Wadsworth Longfellow

Under a spreading chestnut tree
  The village smithy stands;
The smith, a mighty man is he,
  With large and sinewy hands;
And the muscles of his brawny arms
  Are strong as iron bands.

His hair is crisp, and black, and long,
  His face is like the tan;
His brow is wet with honest sweat,
  He earns whate'er he can,
And looks the whole world in the face,

 Habit points from
Laying Down the Rails

For he owes not any man.
Week in, week out, from morn till night,
    You can hear his bellows blow;
You can hear him swing his heavy sledge
    With measured beat and slow,
Like a sexton ringing the village bell,
    When the evening sun is low.

And children coming home from school
    Look in at the open door;
They love to see the flaming forge,
    And hear the bellows roar,
And watch the burning sparks that fly
    Like chaff from a threshing-floor.

He goes on Sunday to the church,
    And sits among his boys;
He hears the parson pray and preach,
    He hears his daughter's voice,
Singing in the village choir,
    And it makes his heart rejoice.

It sounds to him like her mother's voice,
    Singing in Paradise!
He needs must think of her once more,
    How in the grave she lies;
And with his hard, rough hand he wipes
    A tear out of his eyes.

Toiling,—rejoicing,—sorrowing,
    Onward through life he goes;
Each morning sees some task begin,
    Each evening sees it close;
Something attempted, something done,
    Has earned a night's repose.

Thanks, thanks to thee, my worthy friend,
    For the lesson thou hast taught!
Thus at the flaming forge of life
    Our fortunes must be wrought;
Thus on its sounding anvil shaped
    Each burning deed and thought!

Lesson 5

Discuss point four.

 4. Sunday activities are enjoyable and helpful to our bodies and minds.

Read Genesis 2:1–3 to see when God established the need for a restful day. Hebrews 4:1–11 pictures the Sabbath rest that awaits the people of God.

Lesson 6

Talk about point seven.

 7. Sunday activities should leave room for awareness and contemplation of any thoughts God impresses on our minds.

Activity: Instead of adding a new tradition, you could assess your Sunday and take something out of the schedule if you are too busy.

Lesson 7

Talk over point eight and read and discuss the quotation below.

 8. Use appropriate music to help make Sundays pleasant.

> *"In the name of Jesus Christ, who was never in a hurry, we pray, O God, that You will slow us down, for we know that we live too fast. With all of eternity before us, make us take time to live—time to get acquainted with You, time to enjoy You, time to enjoy Your blessings, and time to know each other." — Peter Marshall*

Lesson 8

Have a Parent Share moment to share a story from your life or tell about a person who exemplifies Sunday-Keeping. Read and discuss the quotation below, then finish up with any other discussion, ideas, or celebration your family enjoys. Keep up this habit while going forth to concentrate on a new one.

> *"Sunday is the core of our civilization, dedicated to thought and reverence." — Ralph Waldo Emerson*

5. Make Sundays pleasant in attitude and conversation.

6. Keep a special book that your family reads aloud and shares together only on Sundays; well-chosen poetry would also be appropriate.

Thanksgiving

Being grateful to God for all His blessings

Parent Prep

Read detailed thoughts about Thanksgiving on pages 157 and 158 of *Laying Down the Rails* and skim the lessons below.

◆ Goals for this Habit (and steps to get there)

_____

_____

_____

◆ A Person or Story from My Life that Demonstrates this Habit

_____

_____

_____

◆ Additional Stories, Poems, Quotations, Bible Verses I Want to Use

_____

_____

_____

◆ Other Activities We Could Do to Practice this Habit

_____

_____

_____

◆ Celebration Ideas

_____

_____

_____

Lesson 1

Read the definition and discuss the habit of Thanksgiving. Share with the children any goals you've identified for this habit (for instance, "Each day we will look for things to be thankful for and share them at the supper table.") Also get their input on changes they think need to be made.

Read the Biblical principle found in 1 Thessalonians 5:18 from your preferred version of the Bible. All circumstances are opportunities for a thankful heart.

Lesson 2

Talk about point one, remembering some past answered prayers. Read and discuss the poem that follows.

 1. Give thanks for answered prayer.

A Thanksgiving
by John Kendrick Bangs

For summer rains, and winter's sun,
   For autumn breezes crisp and sweet;
For labors doing, to be done,
   And labors all complete;
For April, May, and lovely June,
   For bud, and bird, and berried vine;
For joys of morning, night, and noon,
   My thanks, dear Lord, are Thine!

For loving friends on every side;
   For children full of joyous glee;
For all the blessed heavens wide,
   And for the sounding sea;
For mountains, valleys, forests deep;
   For maple, oak, and lofty pine;
For rivers on their seaward sweep,
   My thanks, dear Lord, are Thine!

For light and air, for sun and shade,
   For merry laughter and for cheer;
For music and the glad parade
   Of blessings through the year;
For all the fruitful earth's increase,
   For home and life, and love divine,
For hope, and faith, and perfect peace,
   My thanks, dear Lord, are Thine!

Lesson 3

Talk over point two and the quotation.

"Swift gratitude is the sweetest." — Greek proverb

 2. Cultivate a thankful heart all throughout the day as well.

Activity: Every thing, every circumstance can be found to have a positive side to it. Play a game in which you name a person or thing and the children take turns saying what the best thing about that item is. You could add a time limit of several seconds to make it more challenging. Ideas: The Best Thing About . . .

 Habit points from
Laying Down the Rails

- Rain
- My brother or sister
- Being sick in bed
- Doing chores
- School days
- Hot weather
- Going to the doctor/dentist
- Shoes
- Holidays (or choose a specific one, like Christmas or Independence Day)
- Bedtime
- Medicine
- Camping
- Bikes
- My teacher or coach
- Lollipops
- Going to the park
- My birthday
- Traveling
- Eyesight, taste (any of the five senses)
- Our family vehicle

"Now here is a point all parents are not enough awake to—that serious mental and moral ailments require prompt, purposeful, curative treatment, to which the parents must devote themselves for a short time, just as they would to a sick child" (Vol. 2, p. 87).

Lesson 4

Even when amazing things happen to us, we can forget to thank God.

Read Luke 17:11–19. Ten lepers were healed and only one returned to thank Jesus.

Lesson 5

Read and discuss the quotation and fable below.

"A thankful heart is not only the greatest virtue, but the parent of all other virtues."
— *Cicero*

The Plane Tree
adapted from *The Aesop for Children* by Milo Winter

Two Travelers, walking in the noonday sun, sought the shade of a wide-spreading tree to rest. As they lay looking up among the pleasant leaves, they saw that it was a Plane Tree.

"How useless is the Plane!" said one of them. "It bears no fruit whatever, and only serves to litter the ground with leaves."

"Ungrateful creatures!" said a voice from the Plane Tree. "You lie here in my cooling shade, and yet you say I am useless! Thus ungratefully do men receive their blessings!"

Our best blessings are often the least appreciated.

Lesson 6

Read and discuss the quotation.

"The worship most acceptable to God comes from a thankful and cheerful heart."
— *Plato*

Activity: Commit to a one- or two-week time period for starting every day expressing specific thanks to God. You could all state your thanks at breakfast or morning devotions. This starts your day in a thankful mood and acknowledges the Giver of good gifts.

Lesson 7

Take time to express thanksgiving to God in big and little things. Read and discuss "The Eagle."

The Eagle
from *Harper's Third Reader*, edited by James Baldwin

The eagle is one of the largest and strongest birds of prey. Its beak is sharp and strong, and its claws are curved and pointed so that it can seize and hold its prey.

Sometimes the eagle has been known to carry off even young children to its nest. A few years ago this very thing happened in the mountains of Scotland.

It was a pleasant day in summer, and men, women, and children were out in the meadows making hay. A little babe who was too small to do any work lay asleep in the shade of a great rock.

A golden eagle, who had his nest high up on the mountain, saw the child; and while the haymakers were busy at the other end of the field, he swooped down and seized her in his strong claws. The men in the meadow ran towards him, but he spread his great wings and flew up to the top of the mountain, carrying the babe with him.

Some of the men and women tried to climb the steep mountainside; but there was no pathway, and they soon became tired and turned back. But the mother of the babe did not turn back. She knew that the eagle's nest was high above her, and she would not think of giving up until she had reached it and saved her child.

She climbed up steep rocks where no one had ever before dared to go. Her hands were scratched and torn with briers and thorns; her feet were bleeding, being cut by sharp rocks. Yet she did not think of any of these things, for her child was in the eagle's nest.

After some time she came to the nest—a great pile of sticks on the top of a bare rock. Three young eagles were in the nest, and right among them lay the baby fast asleep! The old eagle had flown away again.

In haste the mother caught up her child, and turned to go back down the mountainside. But going down was harder than climbing up. Often she slipped and almost fell down the steep places. There was no path, and she did not know which way to go to reach the meadow in safety.

Just then a sheep with her little lamb passed by. "The sheep knows which way to go," said the mother, "I will follow her." So she took the sheep as her guide, and just as the sun went down behind the mountains, she stood with her babe safe in her arms, among her glad, wondering friends in the meadow.

"Truly," said an old man who had seen it all, "truly, God was with her, to guide her up the steep mountainside and keep all harm out of her way." And men, women, and children knelt down upon the new-mown hay and thanked God for his goodness.

Lesson 8

Use Psalm 136 as an interactive psalm of Thanksgiving. The leader reads the recital while the rest of the group responds with the repeating refrain.

Lesson 9

Have a Parent Share moment to share a story from your life or tell about a person who exemplifies the habit of Thanksgiving, then read and discuss the quotation below.

"Pride slays thanksgiving, but an humble mind is the soil out of which thanks naturally grows. A proud man is seldom a grateful man, for he never thinks he gets as much as he deserves." — *Henry Ward Beecher*

Lesson 10

Finish up with any other discussion, ideas, or celebration your family enjoys. Keep up this habit while going forth to concentrate on a new one.

Thought of God
Thinking rightly about God throughout each day's events

Parent Prep

Read detailed thoughts about Thought of God on pages 159–161 of *Laying Down the Rails* and skim the lessons below.

♦ Goals for this Habit (and steps to get there)

_____

_____

_____

♦ A Person or Story from My Life that Demonstrates this Habit

_____

_____

_____

_____

♦ Additional Stories, Poems, Quotations, Bible Verses I Want to Use

_____

_____

_____

_____

♦ Other Activities We Could Do to Practice this Habit

_____

_____

_____

_____

♦ Celebration Ideas

_____

_____

_____

_____

Lesson 1

Read the definition and discuss Thought of God. Share with the children any goals you've identified for this habit (for instance, "We will look for opportunities to encourage one another with words or notes about God throughout the day.") Also get their input on changes they think need to be made.

Read the Biblical principle found in Colossians 3:1–4 from your preferred version of the Bible. Our minds should dwell on things above not on things here on the earth.

Lesson 2

Discuss point one and read and discuss the poem below.

 1. Direct your thoughts to God whether you are happy, resting, working, or giving.

I Never Saw a Moor
by Emily Dickinson

I never saw a moor,
I never saw the sea;
Yet know I how the heather looks,
And what a wave must be.
I never spoke with God,
Nor visited in heaven;
Yet certain am I of the spot
As if the chart were given.

2. Answer your child's questions about things divine by guiding him into true, happy thinking about God.

Lesson 3

Read and discuss the quotation, then talk over point three.

"Lord, make me see Thy glory in every place." — Michelangelo

 3. An ongoing relationship of love and personal service to God as Heavenly Father and King is most important, rather than just a duty to "be good."

Activity: Have a question/discussion time with your children. Let them ask any questions they have about God. Ask them what they think before you lead them to answers. You could also ask them questions and listen to their thoughts. Children will surprise you with their depth of questions and answers. Don't be afraid to search for answers with them if you don't know what to say. Questions might include

- What does God do all day?
- What does God look like?
- Why did God create the world?
- Could we ever do something so bad, that God can't forgive us?
- Does God ever get tired? hungry? etc.

4. Encouraging this habit of thought of God now will help your child practice the presence of God as an adult.

Lesson 4

Remember the big battle happening in the heavenlies instead of getting stuck in the irritations and worries of earthly life.

Read Ephesians 6:10–20. Our battle isn't against flesh and blood, but against spiritual forces of evil. We use special heavenly gifts to fight this battle.

Habit points from *Laying Down the Rails*

Lesson 5

God cares for us, but He won't force us to acknowledge His presence. Read and discuss the poem, "Overheard in an Orchard."

Overheard in an Orchard
by Elizabeth Cheney

Said the robin to the sparrow,
 "I should really like to know
Why those anxious human beings
 Rush around and worry so."

Said the sparrow to the robin,
 "Friend, I think that it must be
That they have no Heavenly Father
 Such as cares for you and me."

Lesson 6

Read and discuss the quotation below. The habit of Thought of God can lead to being so focused on God that even small things throughout the day remind us of Him and truths about Him.

"Let us not be Christians as to the few great things of our lives, and atheists as to the many small things which fill up a far greater space of them. God is in both, waiting for the glory we can give Him in them." — Dwight L. Moody

Activity: Make reminder cards that contain possible mental connections between God and the tasks we do every day. Print corresponding Scripture verses, including the text as well as the reference, on index cards or decorative paper. Place the cards near the spots the tasks are done. Examples:

- Morning time—Lamentations 3:22, 23
- Washing hands or dishes—Psalm 51:7
- Looking in the mirror—James 1:22–24
- Copywork or other writing exercises—Jeremiah 31:33b
- Meal time—Psalm 136:25, Psalm 145:15, or Matthew 6:25
- Bed time—Psalm 121:3, 4

Lesson 7

Life on earth is short, yet there is something greater to live for which will last beyond the grave. Read and discuss "A Name in the Sand."

A Name in the Sand
by Hannah Flagg Gould

Alone I walked the ocean strand;
A pearly shell was in my hand:
I stooped and wrote upon the sand

My name—the year—the day.
As onward from the spot I passed,
One lingering look behind I cast;
A wave came rolling high and fast,
    And washed my lines away.

And so, methought, 't will shortly be
With every mark on earth from me:
A wave of dark oblivion's sea
    Will sweep across the place
Where I have trod the sandy shore
Of time, and been, to be no more,
Of me—my day—the name I bore,
    To leave nor track nor trace.

And yet, with Him who counts the sands
And holds the waters in His hands,
I know a lasting record stands
    Inscribed against my name,
Of all this mortal part has wrought,
Of all this thinking soul has thought,
And from these fleeting moments caught
    For glory or for shame.

Lesson 8

Relate the following Scriptures to Thought of God.

> Philippians 4:8—Keep your mind on good things.
> Hebrews 12:1–3—Think on Jesus.
> Mark 12:28–34—Love the Lord your God with all your heart.
> James 4:6–10—Come near to God.

Lesson 9

Hebrews 12:1 talks about the great cloud of witnesses that surrounds us, encouraging us to continue in the faith. Read and discuss the poem, "A Psalm of Life."

A Psalm of Life
by Henry Wadsworth Longfellow

Tell me not, in mournful numbers,
    Life is but an empty dream!—
For the soul is dead that slumbers,
    And things are not what they seem.

Life is real! Life is earnest!
    And the grave is not its goal;
Dust thou art, to dust returnest,

Was not spoken of the soul.

Not enjoyment, and not sorrow,
　　Is our destined end or way;
But to act, that each tomorrow
　　Find us farther than today.

Art is long, and Time is fleeting,
　　And our hearts, though stout and brave,
Still, like muffled drums, are beating
　　Funeral marches to the grave.

In the world's broad field of battle,
　　In the bivouac of Life,
Be not like dumb, driven cattle!
　　Be a hero in the strife!

Trust no Future, howe'er pleasant!
　　Let the dead Past bury its dead!
Act,—act in the living Present!
　　Heart within, and God o'erhead!

Lives of great men all remind us
　　We can make our lives sublime,
And, departing, leave behind us
　　Footprints on the sands of time;

Footprints, that perhaps another,
　　Sailing o'er life's solemn main,
A forlorn and shipwrecked brother,
　　Seeing, shall take heart again.

Let us, then, be up and doing,
　　With a heart for any fate;
Still achieving, still pursuing,
　　Learn to labor and to wait.

Lesson 10

Have a Parent Share moment to share a story from your life or tell about a person who exemplifies the habit of Thought of God. Read and discuss the poem below, then finish up with any other discussion, ideas, or celebration your family enjoys. Keep up this habit while going forth to concentrate on a new one.

Lord, purge our eyes to see
Within the seed a tree,
Within the glowing egg a bird,
Within the shroud a butterfly:

Till taught by such, we see
Beyond all creatures, Thee, . . . — Christina Rossetti

Habits Index